NAVIGATION

NAVIGATION

An RYA Manual

ROYAL YACHTING ASSOCIATION
in association with

DAVID & CHARLES
Newton Abbot   London   North Pomfret (Vt)

British Library Cataloguing in Publication Data

Navigation.
  1. Navigation
  2. Yachts and yachting
  I. Royal Yachting Association

623.89'0247971   VK555

ISBN (hardback edition) 0 7153 8246 2
ISBN (paperback edition) 0 7153 8258 6

Typeset by Typesetters (Birmingham) Ltd
and printed in Great Britain
by Ebenezer Baylis & Son Ltd,
The Trinity Press, Worcester, and London
for David & Charles (Publishers) Limited
Brunel House Newton Abbot Devon

Published in the United States of America
by David & Charles Inc
North Pomfret Vermont 05053 USA

Contents

List of Illustrations

Figures

    (photographs courtesy of Henry Browne & Son Ltd)

Colour plates

Keys

Introduction

This book has been written in response to demand for a work on navigation which covers the syllabus for the Yachtmaster Offshore Certificate.

There are two possible approaches to navigation: the mathematical, which treats problems essentially as a matter of calculating the shortest distance between two points on an oblate spheroid (the squashed sphere which we inhabit), and the graphical, which encourages the solution of problems by drawing lines on charts. The former is best suited to commercial and ocean navigation, when the saving of fuel is of paramount importance. The latter, upon which this book is based, is appropriate to yachts, as most of the errors which can be made are apparent to anyone with common sense and the graphical representation on a chart is relatively easy to relate to the physical geography of the sea and coastline.

A number of aspects of navigation must be learned and understood by the prospective navigator: these include certain facts, such as the conventions of chart symbols and of buoyage; the techniques of working on charts, with the application of simple geometry to plot positions and predict courses; the ability to predict tidal heights and tidal-stream rates and directions; and a knowledge of the publications which provide navigational information and the instruments which are available as aids to navigation. All of these aspects can be acquired, in theory, in the classroom or from books. They are the essential facts upon which navigation is based and they are all important, but a knowledge of them does not necessarily make a navigator.

The ability to draw and calculate accurately is important. Gross factual errors destroy navigation. Approximations adopted for their simplicity reduce navigational accuracy and the amount by which they do so may or may not be important. Short-cut methods are perfectly allowable, even desirable, in a yacht where working conditions are difficult and time spent at the chart table reduces general sailing efficiency. However, the decision to use short-cut methods must be taken consciously, with a full knowledge of the accuracy sacrificed or the risk of gross error introduced. This decision can be taken only by the navigator who fully understands the techniques and processes involved. This is the reason why this book encourages an understanding of some methods and techniques which have an inherent accuracy in excess of that which will be achievable in a yacht at sea. An understanding of the most accurate methods available allows the navigator to estimate the magnitude of the inaccuracies which he is introducing by using approximations.

Good navigation can be achieved only by experience. Imaginary passages, worked on the dining-room table, help to build up speed and proficiency in chart-work, but they cannot be a substitute for practice at sea. The physical problems of taking accurate bearings, steering compass courses, measuring distance run and working on a chart table are liable to discourage the learner who has acquired a knowledge of navigational theory. Practice does not make the waves any smaller, the driving spray less penetrating or the motion less violent, but it teaches the navigator to come to terms with the problems which are a part of sea-going in yachts. The art of steadying a gyrating hand-bearing compass, finding a comfortable working position at a chart table heeled to an angle of 45° and estimating the amount the helmsman steers to windward of his course on a reach are just as important as the subjects covered in this book. They cannot be taught by lecturers or writers, only by the sea.

1 Chart-work

The process of conducting a yacht safely from one harbour to another involves a combination of the skills of seamanship and navigation. Chart-work is that part of navigation concerned with constructing lines and measuring distances on the chart to lay-off courses, fixing positions and keeping track of the yacht's progress. These techniques involve an understanding of charts and the information which they portray in the form of symbols and abbreviations. They also require proficient use of various navigational drawing instruments. It is therefore with charts, instruments and the basic navigational definitions that the subject of chart-work is introduced.

Definitions

Position
The position of any point on the Earth's surface can be indicated in terms of the co-ordinates of latitude and longitude. Charts are overprinted with a lattice of parallels of latitude and meridians of longitude to enable the navigator to plot or take off positions.

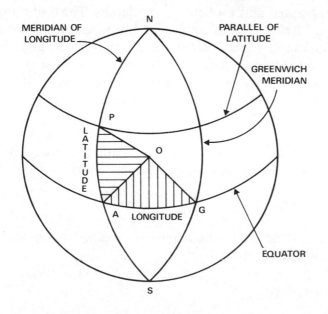

Fig 1.1 Latitude and Longitude

The latitude of a position is the angular distance, measured along the meridian, from 0° to 90° north or south of the equator. The longitude of a position is the arc of the equator from the Greenwich meridian to the meridian of the position, measured from 0° to 180° east or west from Greenwich. In Fig 1.1 the latitude of P is the angular distance AP and the longitude is the angular distance GA.

Latitude and longitude are measured in degrees (°), minutes ('), and seconds ("). There are 60 minutes in a degree and 60 seconds in a minute. Where extreme accuracy is required, a position may be given in terms of degrees, minutes and seconds, eg, Eddystone Lighthouse: 50°10'48"N 4°15'52"W. For normal navigational purposes this degree of accuracy is unnecessary and positions are given in degrees, minutes and tenths of a minute,. eg, Eddystone Lighthouse: 50°10'.8N 4°15'.9W.

Distance

The unit of distance used in navigation is the sea mile. It is defined as the length of 1 minute of arc, measured along the meridian, in the latitude of the position. Its actual length varies slightly with latitude but it is about 1,853m (6,080ft). In practice, it is an extremely simple unit to use because it is the length of 1 minute of latitude. (The international nautical mile which is used for scientific purposes to define distance with precision is a distance of 1,852m. It is about the same distance as the sea mile but has no general use in navigation.)

A cable is one tenth of a sea mile (approximately 600ft) and is written as a decimal, eg, 6 miles and 3 cables is written as 6·3M.

The statute mile of 1,760yd is never used in navigation. Any reference to miles at sea can therefore be assumed to be sea miles.

The metre is now the accepted unit for heights and depths. The traditional units of fathoms (6ft) and feet may be encountered, but with the increasing acceptance of metrication they are fading from the navigational vocabulary.

It is important to remember that the standard abbreviation for sea miles is 'M' and for metres 'm', as confusion between the two can easily arise. It may help to remember that the larger unit has the larger abbreviation.

Speed

The unit of speed is the knot, which is a velocity of 1 sea mile per hour. There is a simple but very important relationship between time, speed and distance:

$$\text{Speed (knots)} = \frac{\text{Distance (sea miles)}}{\text{Time (hours)}}$$

This formula may be used to find speed when time and distance are known or to find distance when speed and time are known.

Example 1.1
A yacht sails 15·5M in 3 hours 42 minutes. What is her speed?

$$\text{Speed} = \frac{15 \cdot 5}{3 \cdot 7} = 4 \cdot 2 \text{ knots.}$$

Example 1.2
A yacht sails at a speed of 6·5 knots for 3 hours 30 minutes. What distance has she sailed?

$$\text{Distance} = 6 \cdot 5 \times 3 \cdot 5 = 22 \cdot 75 \text{M.}$$

Direction
Direction is measured with reference to North and is expressed in terms of courses and bearings. The course is the direction from one position to another. A bearing is the direction of an object from an observer, with reference to North.

The standard method of measuring direction is three-figure notation in degrees, clockwise from 000° (North) to 359°. Other notations will be encountered, for example, points notation which is primarily used to indicate wind direction (Fig 1.2).

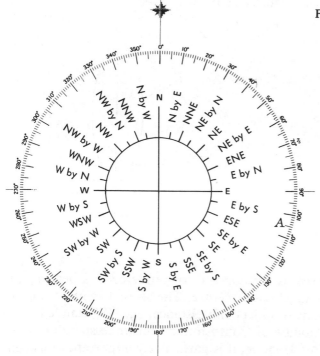

Fig 1.2 The 360° and 32 point notation

The fact that the world is round means that the most direct course from one point to another or the observed bearing of a distant object is a line which would appear as a curve on a chart drawn on a Mercator projection (see below). The most convenient form of line to use for navigation is a rhumb line, a line which cuts all meridians at the same angle and which appears on a Mercator projection as a straight line. The rhumb line differs by so little from a true shortest-distance straight line over distances up to 100 miles that there is no significant loss of accuracy in assuming that all courses and bearings are rhumb lines. The true shortest-distance straight line, which is known as a great circle, is only of practical navigational significance when very long distances are involved.

A relative bearing is the direction of an object expressed with reference to the direction of ship's head instead of North. It is particularly useful for describing the direction of another vessel, as relative bearings are more easily appreciated than bearings which require the use of North as a reference point (Fig 1.3).

Fig 1.3 Relative direction

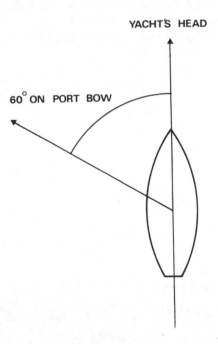

Indicating Position
A position may be expressed as latitude and longitude or as a bearing and distance *from* a conspicuous charted feature. The second method may be abbreviated to bearing, name of object and distance, eg, 118° Randell Point 17M. To avoid the possibility of confusion or misunderstanding when passing a position by radio-telephone, it is particularly important to use one of the standard methods.

Tidal Streams

There is a special terminology for speed, distance and direction applied to tidal streams. The speed is known as rate (in knots); the total distance moved owing to the influence of the tidal stream over a period of time is the drift (in sea miles), and the direction towards which the tidal stream is flowing is the set.

By convention, tidal streams flow towards a direction but winds blow from a direction.

Chart-work Instruments

Four basic navigational drawing instruments are recommended for the beginner: parallel rules, dividers, pencil compasses and the Douglas protractor. Other more complex instruments, which are a combination of a drawing instrument and a simple analogue computer, are favoured by some experienced navigators. However, anyone who can use the basic instruments will have little difficulty adapting to the more complex ones.

Parallel rules are used to measure direction on the chart. The perspex type, graduated as a protractor, are the easiest to use and they should be of a size suitable for the size of the chart table in the yacht in which they are to be used. In general, the longer the rules the easier they are to use, but on a small chart table long rules are extremely inconvenient. Rolling rules are available and they are excellent for working on an absolutely flat and steady table but they cannot be recommended for use in yachts (Fig 1.4).

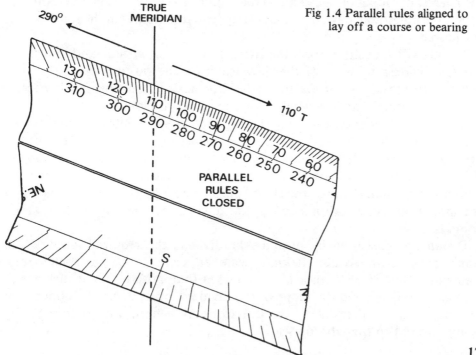

Fig 1.4 Parallel rules aligned to lay off a course or bearing

Dividers are used to measure distance on the chart. They may be straight or bow type, depending on personal preference. It is worth investing in a large robust pair.

Pencil compasses are useful for drawing in ranges and for construction on the chart.

The Douglas protractor is a square of transparent perspex material, graduated around the edge from 0° to 359° as a protractor, with horizontal and vertical lines to align the protractor on the chart. It combines the functions of parallel rule and protractor and is particularly useful in small boats where the chart table is likely to be small and possibly not rigidly mounted.

Two hexagonal B or 2B-grade pencils and soft rubbers complete the essential navigational drawing instruments.

Parallel rules and dividers
All working on the chart should be tidy and neat to avoid the mistakes which inevitably result from untidy chart-work. Pencil lines should be clear without being unkind to the chart. Never rub out pencil lines on a wet chart as the printing also will be removed.

To plot a position from its latitude and longitude, first line up the rules along the nearest parallel of latitude and then 'walk' them to the required point on the latitude scale. Draw a pencil line in the vicinity of the required longitude. Then with the dividers step off the exact distance required from the nearest meridian on the chart to the required longitude (Fig 1.5). Alternatively, the longitude may be plotted using the parallel rules in the same way as for latitude.

To take off a position from the chart, in terms of latitude and longitude, use the dividers to step off the distance from the position to the nearest parallel of latitude and refer to the latitude scale. Then, using the nearest meridian of longitude in a similar way, read off the longitude.

To measure a course or bearing, line up the parallel rules with the compass rose or a meridian of longitude. The latter method involves the use of the protractor on the rules and may entail a little simple mathematics to convert the 360° notation to the protractor graduations, but it is likely to reduce the amount of 'walking' across the chart. There is always a convenient meridian available near the working area but not always such a conveniently placed compass rose.

Distance is measured by opening the dividers the required amount and transferring them to the latitude scale adjacent to the working area. Remember that 1′ of latitude is 1 sea mile at that latitude. If the distance to be measured is beyond the scope of the dividers, open them to a convenient distance and step them along the line to be measured, any balance finally being referred to the latitude scale.

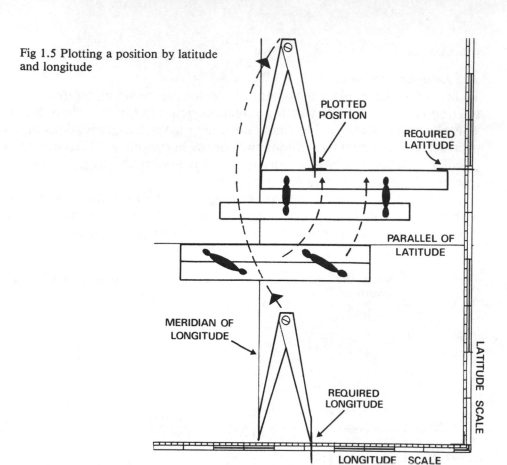

Fig 1.5 Plotting a position by latitude and longitude

PLOTTED POSITION

REQUIRED LATITUDE

PARALLEL OF LATITUDE

MERIDIAN OF LONGITUDE

REQUIRED LONGITUDE

LONGITUDE SCALE

LATITUDE SCALE

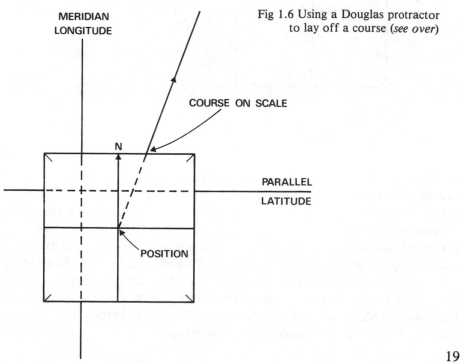

MERIDIAN LONGITUDE

Fig 1.6 Using a Douglas protractor to lay off a course (*see over*)

COURSE ON SCALE

N

PARALLEL LATITUDE

POSITION

19

The Douglas Protractor

To lay off a course, place the protractor on the chart with its centre over the starting position and the North graduation pointing towards chart North. This alignment is achieved by lining up either the vertical graduations on the protractor with a meridian of longitude or the horizontal graduations with a parallel of latitude. Mark off the required course at the edge of the protractor using the outer ring of figures (Fig 1.6).

To measure a charted course or bearing align the protractor, North up, with the centre of the protractor on the course or bearing line. Read off the direction of the course or bearing line from the outer ring of figures (Fig 1.7).

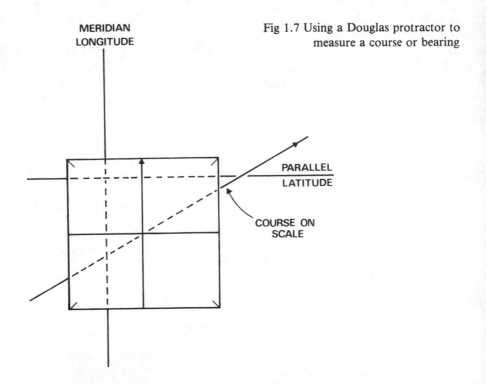

MERIDIAN
LONGITUDE

Fig 1.7 Using a Douglas protractor to measure a course or bearing

PARALLEL
LATITUDE

COURSE ON
SCALE

When plotting the bearing of a terrestrial object, remember that the bearing is observed from seaward towards the object. Using a Douglas protractor the only bearing which it is possible to plot is the reciprocal, the bearing of the observer from the object. This can be achieved by placing the centre of the protractor over the object with the North point on the protractor aligned with chart South and marking off the observed bearing on the outer ring of figures (Fig 1.8). Alternatively, the protractor can be used in the conventional North-up position if the reciprocal of the observed bearing is first calculated, by adding or subtracting 180°. The protractor may also be used to plot horizontal angles (see Chapter 4).

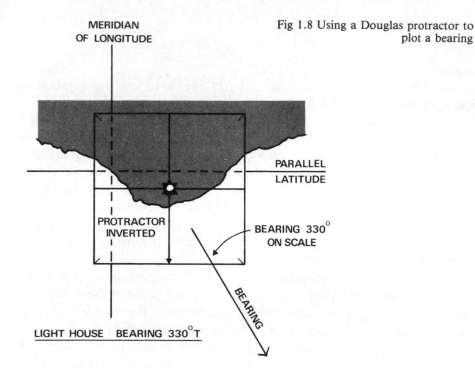

MERIDIAN
OF LONGITUDE

Fig 1.8 Using a Douglas protractor to plot a bearing

PARALLEL
LATITUDE

PROTRACTOR
INVERTED

BEARING 330°
ON SCALE

BEARING

LIGHT HOUSE BEARING 330°T

Standard Chart-work Symbols

The navigation of a yacht may be carried out by a number of people working in different watches. It is much easier for the oncoming watch to pick up the threads if standard chart-work symbols which are familiar to everyone are used. The accepted conventions are illustrated in Fig 1.9.

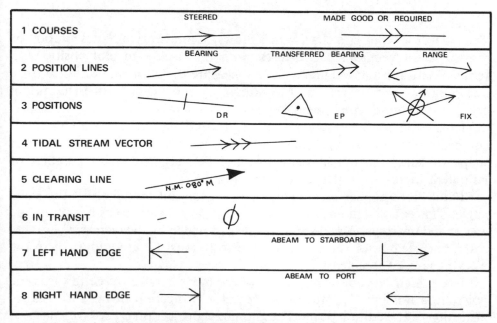

Fig 1.9 Conventional chartwork symbols (7 and 8 are used in a log or notebook rather than on the chart)

Charts

Suppliers

Responsibility for world-wide charting is regulated by the International Hydrographic Bureau. Each of the major maritime nations accepts responsibility as the primary charting authority for its own coastline and adjacent waters, and in some cases for those of its historic dependencies. The UK is one of the few countries which publishes a series of charts giving worldwide coverage. Admiralty charts are published by the Hydrographic Department of the Ministry of Defence (Navy) and distributed by Admiralty chart agents.

The *Admiralty Catalogue of Charts* is published annually and gives details of all the Hydrographic Department charts and navigational publications. A home edition of the catalogue (NP109), covering northern European waters, is particularly useful to yachtsmen.

Admiralty charts are the most detailed and comprehensive available for the UK coast and they are adequate for most other areas of the world. However, if particularly detailed charts of foreign coasts are required, especially where the topography has a marked unique national characteristic, such as the Norwegian fiords, the Swedish archipelago or the Dutch inland waterways, it is preferable, and sometimes essential, to use the charts of those countries.

Two publishing companies, Imray, Laurie, Norie & Wilson Ltd and Stanford Maritime Ltd also produce a very limited series of charts for yachtsmen. Both series are based mainly on the Admiralty charts and are distributed through chandlers and bookshops.

Projections

The navigator requires a chart which shows an undistorted representation of the shapes of geographical features, with the facility to plot positions in terms of latitude and longitude and to measure direction and distance from one position to another. The Mercator projection (Fig 1.10) is unique in achieving all these requirements.

The meridians are drawn as equally spaced parallel straight lines. To compensate for this straightening of the meridians and maintain the correct shape of land, the north–south distance between successive parallels of latitude is increased in the same proportion.

Rhumb lines appear as straight lines, cutting all meridians at the same angle. This enables the navigator to lay off and measure easily rhumb-line course and bearings. A scale of distance is provided by the increasing latitude scale, but because of the distortion the scale must be used adjacent to the working area of the chart.

In very high latitudes (over 70°), where meridians converge towards the poles, it is not practical to use a Mercator projection owing to excessive distortion of the latitude scale. The gnomonic projection is used for charts of

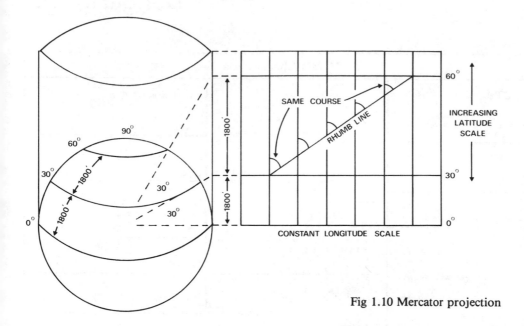

Fig 1.10 Mercator projection

polar regions and for some small-scale charts of ocean areas. Meridians of longitude are drawn as straight lines converging towards the poles and parallels of latitude appear as curves (Fig 1.11). Great-circle tracks appear as straight lines and this facilitates the planning of long ocean passages in which the great-circle distance is significantly shorter than the rhumb line.

Harbour plans and very large-scale charts are drawn on gnomonic or transverse Mercator projections, but for charts of such large scale the projection used has no practical significance.

Fig 1.11 Gnomonic projection

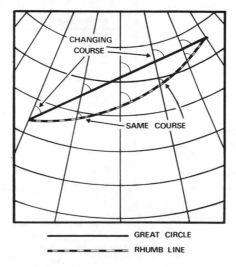

Metric Charts

1 Rock which does not cover (with elevation above MHWS or MHHW, or where there is no tide, above MSL)

(4) **(4)** **(4)** **.(0·6)**

2 §Rock which covers and uncovers (with elevation above chart datum)

Dries 1·2m **Dr 1·2m** **(1₂)**

3 Rock awash at the level of chart datum

4 Underwater rock with 2 metres or less water over it at chart datum, or

rock ledge on which depths are known to be 2 metres or less, or

a rock or rock ledge over which the exact depth is unknown but which is considered to be dangerous to surface navigation

5 Shoal sounding on isolated rock

10₇ R   16₅ R

6 Underwater rock not dangerous to surface navigation

35 R

6a Underwater danger with depth cleared by wire drag sweep

6₄   11₂

(Oc) Restricted area round the site of a wreck of historical and archaeological importance.

Historic Wreck (see Note)   Historic Wreck (see Note)

10 §Coral reef

(Covers and uncovers)   (Always covered)

11 Wreck showing any portion of hull or super-structure at the level of chart datum

Wk
Large scale charts

12 Wreck of which the masts only are visible

(Masts)   (Mast 3m)   (Funnel)   (Mast dries 2·1m)
Large scale charts

(Oa) Unsurveyed wreck over which the exact depth is unknown but which is considered to have a safe clearance at the depth shown

15 Wk

14 Wreck over which the exact depth of water is unknown but is thought to be 28 metres or less, and which is considered dangerous to surface navigation

15 ‡Wreck over which the depth has been obtained by sounding, but not by wire sweep

7₃ Wk   7₃ Wk
Large scale charts

15a ‡Wreck which has been swept by wire to the depth shown

9₁ Wk

16 ‡Wreck over which the exact depth is unknown but thought to be more than 28 metres, or

a wreck over which the depth is thought to be 28 metres or less, but which is not considered dangerous to surface vessels capable of navigating in the vicinity.

17 The remains of a wreck, or other foul area, no longer dangerous to surface navigation, but to be avoided by vessels anchoring, trawling, etc.

Foul   Foul
† Foul   22, Foul
Where depth known

18 Overfalls and tide-rips

19 Eddies

20 Kelp

21	Bk.	Bank
22	Sh.	Shoal
23	Rf.	Reef
24	Le.	Ledge

25 Breakers

(Od) Submerged wellhead (with least depth where known)

Well   35 Well

27 Obstruction or danger to navigation the exact nature of which is not specified or has not been determined.

Obstn

28	Wk	Wreck
29	See 17	Wreckage
29a	See 17	Wreck remains
30	See 17	Submerged piling
30a	See 17	Snags; submerged stumps
32	dr	Dries
33	cov	Covers
34	uncov	Uncovers
35	Rep † Repd	Reported

38 Limiting danger line

1₃   9₁

(Ob) Areas of mobile bottom (including sand waves)

41	PA	†(PA)	Position approximate
42	PD	†(PD)	Position doubtful
43	ED	†(ED)	Existence doubtful
		See Q1	Sounding of doubtful depth
44	pos	†posn	Position
46	unexam †unexamd		Unexamined

§ See note on Drying Heights given in the Introduction

‡ Where the depth of a wreck exceeds 28 metres, or where a wreck is otherwise considered non-dangerous, the corresponding symbol is generally shown on the largest scale chart only.

† This symbol and/or abbreviation is obsolescent

Information on Admiralty Charts

It is important that the navigator is familiar with the information presented on the chart and is able to 'read' the chart to extract the details he requires. Most of the information is supplied in the form of symbols and abbreviations and he should be familiar with the more important ones (see opposite). A full list of symbols and abbreviations is provided in the Hydrographic Department's publication *Symbols and Abbreviations* (Chart 5011).

Chart Scales

The natural scale of a chart is the relationship between the distance on the chart and the distance on the Earth's surface for a particular latitude. For instance, 1:200,000 means that 1 unit of distance on the chart represents 200,000 units on the Earth's surface. There are three main groups of chart scales: harbour plans, on a very large scale (typically around 1:5,000) covering a very small area in great detail; coastal charts, which show a fair amount of detail of anything between about 10 and 200 miles of coastline; and ocean charts, which cover large areas of the world and are used primarily for passage planning and ocean navigation.

General Information on Charts

Every navigational chart contains information about the surveys on which it is based, the date on which it was compiled and the corrections which have been inserted on it. There is a standard form for the presentation of this type of information, which appears on all charts (Fig 1.12).

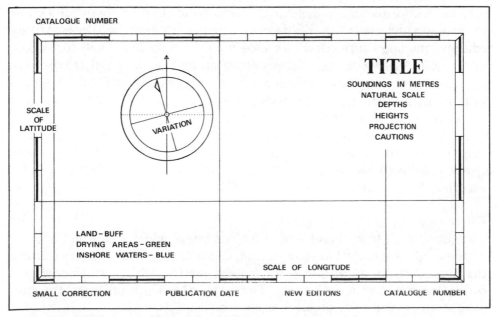

Fig 1.12 Layout of information and reference numbers on Admiralty charts

The catalogue number, printed in the top-right and bottom-left corners and on the thumb label on the back of the chart, simply provides a reference number. There is no logical sequence to these catalogue numbers.

The title of the chart, which is a brief description of the area covered, is printed where it will cause the least interference with navigational information. Under the title are shown the units of depths and heights, natural scale, projection, sources of information and any cautions about the area which should be brought to the attention of the navigator.

The majority of charts of northern Europe use metres as the units of depths and heights, but some charts still use feet or fathoms and feet. It is important to check what units are shown whenever a chart is used.

The form of acknowledgement of source information varies. At its simplest, it may be the date of the survey and the names of the surveying ship and her commanding officer. Where a number of surveys have been used a small plan may be provided to indicate the dates of the surveys used for each area of the chart. This information is important because charts are frequently published on the basis of surveys carried out up to 100 years ago. Until the 1930s echo-sounders were not available and depths were found by the lead and line, or a mechanical version of it. This imposed a limitation on the number of soundings which could be recorded and in rocky areas there was a possibility of missing an isolated pinnacle. Charts based on old surveys should therefore be treated with caution; the original survey may not have been as complete as it would have been with modern equipment and changes may have taken place in the intervening years.

In the margin at the bottom of the chart there are several numbers which give more information on the extent to which the chart has been brought up to date. In the centre is the date of original publication. Dates of new editions and large corrections are shown on the right and small corrections on the left. A new edition or large correction involves a complete reprint of the chart from up-dated printing plates, whereas a small correction is inserted by a chart agent or navigator and does not involve any changes to the plates from which the chart is printed.

The overall dimensions of the chart are also shown in the bottom right-hand corner. When absolute precision is required, the user can use these to check that there has been no distortion of the paper — but this is for accuracy far in excess of anything possible in a yacht.

Depths and Heights
The soundings (depths) and drying heights (areas which cover and uncover with the tide) are related to chart datum. Chart datum on all modern charts is the lowest astronomical tide — the lowest level to which the tide will fall owing to astronomical influences. Thus, the least depth of water, the most hazardous navigational situation is shown.

Depths and drying heights are indicated by spot soundings and the general shape of the sea bed is indicated by depth-contour lines. Colour is used to draw attention to the most important depth-contour lines; green for drying areas and blue for shallow water.

Charted heights are shown above the level of mean high-water springs (MHWS). The relationship between the various levels and datums is shown in Fig 1.13.

The heights of mean tidal levels for the more important ports covered by a chart are tabulated.

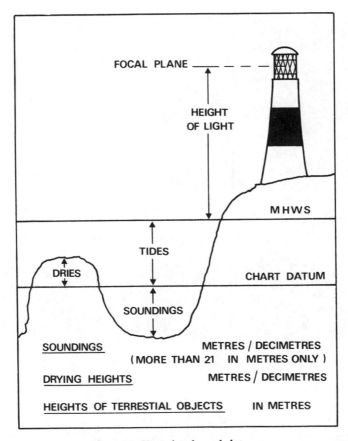

Fig 1.13 Chart levels and datums

Tidal-stream Information

Information about the set and rate of the tidal stream is shown for a number of positions, each position being indicated by a letter enclosed in a diamond. The letter is referred to a table of set and rate for each hour before and after high water at a standard port (Fig 1.14, overleaf).

27

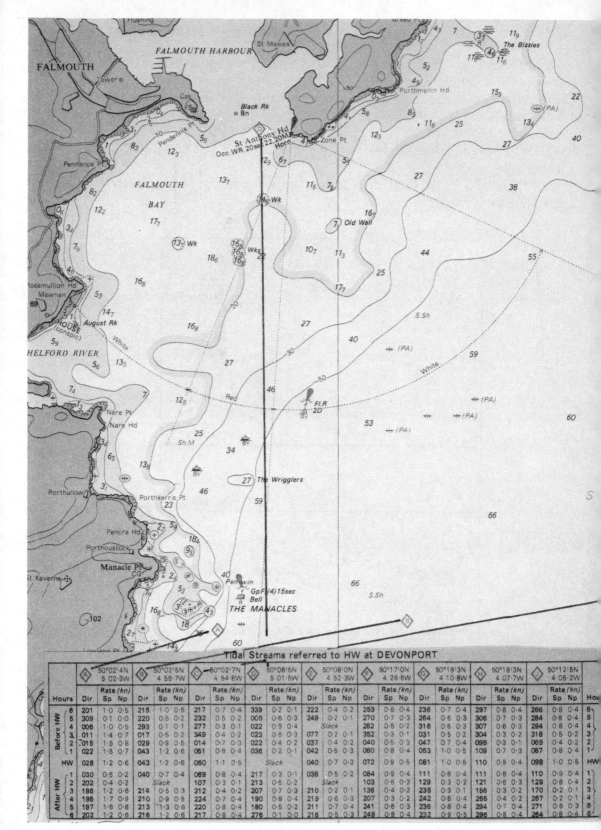

Fig 1.14 Charted tidal stream information

Application of Variation and Deviation
True direction is measured relative to the meridians, true North being the direction towards the geographic North Pole. Unfortunately, there is no instrument available to the yacht navigator which gives a direct indication of the direction of true North. A magnetic compass aligns itself with the magnetic meridians.

Variation
Variation is the angular difference between the true and magnetic meridians. Variation changes both with position and time. At present the magnetic North Pole is situated to the west of the geographic North Pole when measured from the vicinity of the British Isles and is therefore named west. The angle is also decreasing very slowly owing to the movement of the magnetic pole.

The value of variation for an area is shown inside the compass rose on the chart, in the form 'Variation 8°55′ W (1979) decreasing about 5′ annually'. Alternatively, it may be obtained from a variation chart which shows lines joining places with equal values of variation (isogonic lines).

The difference between a true bearing and a magnetic bearing is shown in fig 1.15.

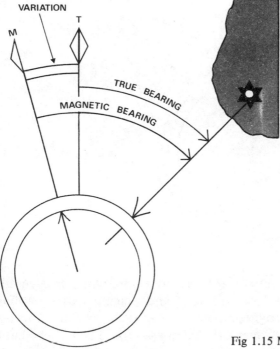

Fig 1.15 Magnetic and true bearings

29

Deviation

The compass needle aligns itself to the magnetic field by which it is influenced. In a yacht this field has two components: the Earth's magnetic field and the magnetic field created by any ferrous metal or electrical equipment in the yacht herself. Deviation is the angle by which the compass needle is deviated from the magnetic meridian by the magnetic influence of the yacht. The value of deviation depends upon the amount of magnetic material in the yacht, the distance between this material and the compass and the heading of the yacht. It is named East or West, depending upon the side of the magnetic meridian towards which the compass needle has been deflected (Fig 1.16).

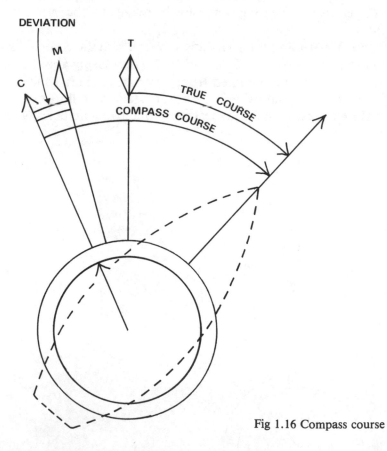

Fig 1.16 Compass course

Deviation can and should be reduced to a minimum, or even eliminated completely, by 'swinging the compass' and placing corrector magnets to counteract the yacht's magnetic field. In any yacht in which there is a substantial amount of ferrous metal the compass should be adjusted at the start of each season because the magnetic properties of metal are subject to slow and continuous change. After the compass has been adjusted, the residual deviation is tabulated, either as a table or as a curve, so that the magnetic heading can be calculated (Fig 1.17). Deviations are found initially for compass headings, but once the curve has been drawn it is relatively simple to calculate and tabulate deviations which apply to magnetic headings.

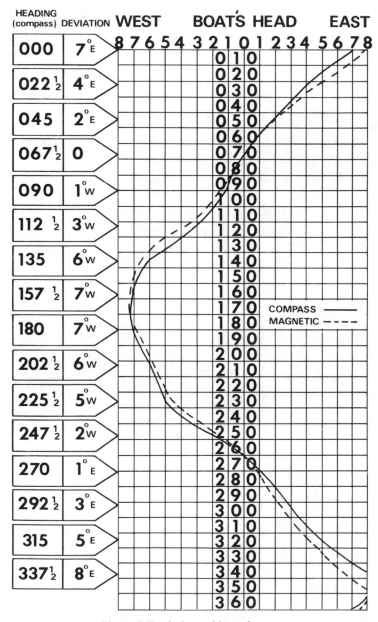

Fig 1.17 Deviation table and curve

Application of Variation and Deviation

The application of variation and deviation follows a rule that, when converting from compass through magnetic to true, 'Add east, subtract west'. Conversely, when working from true through magnetic to compass, 'Add west, subtract east'. The mnemonics **C AD E T** — Compass, **AD**d **E**ast, **T**rue — or the phrase 'Error west compass best, error east compass least', may be useful.

The order of working to convert between compass and true is also important and must be:

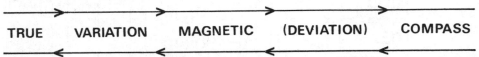

| TRUE | VARIATION | MAGNETIC | (DEVIATION) | COMPASS |

The reason for this rule is that deviation does not relate to true heading and can only be applied to a magnetic or compass heading. The sum of variation and deviation is known as compass error.

Examples of the calculations involved are:

1.3   Magnetic bearing obtained   059°(M)
       Variation from the chart   9°W
       True bearing to plot   050°(T)
       (Fig 1.18)

Fig 1.18

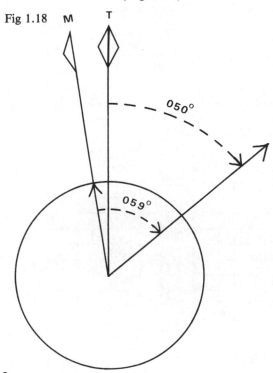

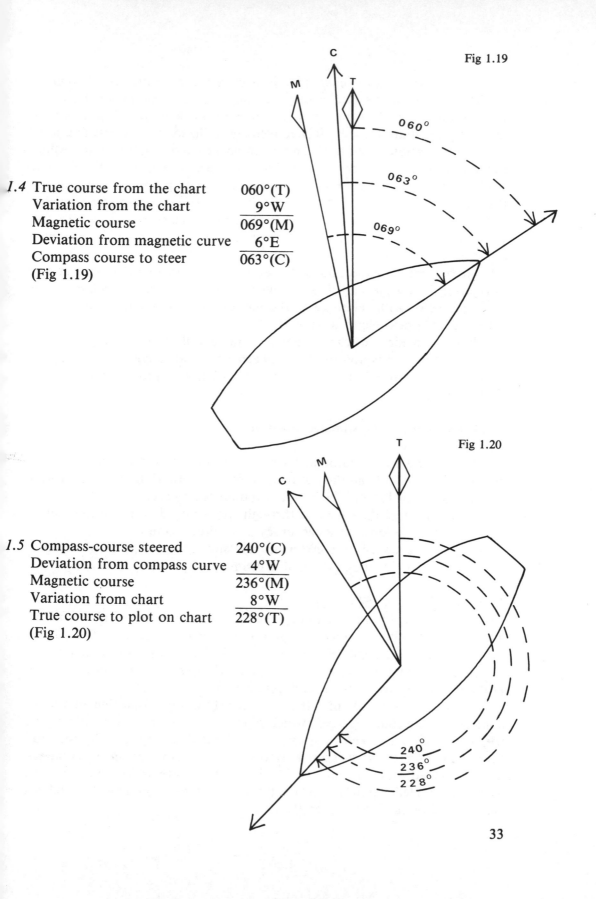

Fig 1.19

1.4 True course from the chart   060°(T)
    Variation from the chart   9°W
    Magnetic course   069°(M)
    Deviation from magnetic curve   6°E
    Compass course to steer   063°(C)
    (Fig 1.19)

Fig 1.20

1.5 Compass-course steered   240°(C)
    Deviation from compass curve   4°W
    Magnetic course   236°(M)
    Variation from chart   8°W
    True course to plot on chart   228°(T)
    (Fig 1.20)

When working on the chart greater accuracy can be obtained laying off and measuring courses and bearings relative to the true meridians. However, it is common practice among yachtsmen to work with reference to the magnetic meridian. It is certainly convenient to do so, particularly in a yacht in which deviation is negligible and when using a plotting instrument which automatically allows for variation. There is nothing 'wrong' with opting to work always in magnetic, but there are a number of points to weigh against the apparent simplicity of this option: the magnetic compass rose is correct only for the date shown and the change in the value of variation with time will therefore introduce a small error; the graduations on the magnetic compass rose are small and difficult to read; the set of the tidal stream is tabulated true; light sectors and leading lines shown on charts and in navigational publications are always named true; if the parallel rules are used as a protractor with reference to the meridians or a Douglas protractor is used it is only possible to work true.

Whether working in true or magnetic there will always be occasions on which it is necessary to convert between true and magnetic or compass. Initially, these conversions may seem tedious but with practice they become almost instinctive.

Dead Reckoning and Estimated Position

Dead Reckoning

Dead reckoning is the traditional term used for the process of working up the position of a vessel from the last reliable fix. By definition, it is the position deduced from the log and the compass and takes into account only two facts: course steered and distance run through the water. It can indicate future approximate positions but its accuracy is inevitably limited.

For greater accuracy, the effect of tidal stream and wind must be taken into account to give the best possible estimate of position.

Estimated Position (EP)

An estimated position is derived by taking into consideration all the factors which it is possible to measure or estimate which influence the yacht's progress over the ground. Next to the fix, it is the most reliable indication of position. Keeping an accurate EP plot requires practice and frequent evaluation of its accuracy against reliable fixes.

In working up an EP plot there are nearly always four elements to be considered; the course steered (which must not be assumed to be the course the helmsman was asked to steer); the estimated leeway; the distance run through the water, as measured by the log with any known or estimated errors applied; the set and drift of the tidal stream or current. The information needed to work up an estimated position should be recorded in a suitable log-book (see Chapter 7).

Leeway

Leeway is the angle between the direction of the yacht's heading and the direction in which she is moving through the water (Fig 1.21). In strong winds with steep seas, leeway angles up to 20° are not uncommon. Leeway is applied as an angle to the direction of the yacht's heading. Any effect the wind has on speed should be accounted for in the distance actually recorded by the log.

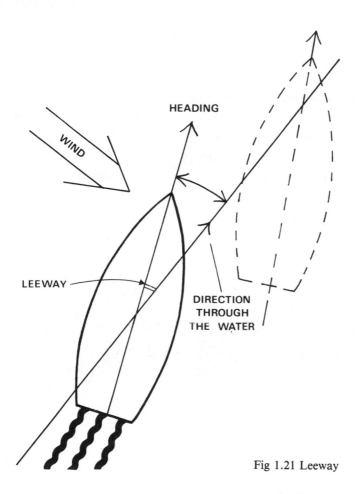

Fig 1.21 Leeway

The factors which affect the amount of leeway made by any yacht are: her hull design, particularly her draught; the amount of windage of her hull, superstructure and rigging; the point of sailing (leeway is a maximum when close-hauled and zero when running or motoring head to wind); the angle of heel (the draught and efficiency of the keel decrease as the angle increases); the strength of wind and the sea state.

35

A rough estimate of leeway can be made by taking a bearing along the line of the wake and comparing this with the reciprocal of the compass heading. Unfortunately, this gives much better results in calm weather than in rough, when the compass heading is seldom steady for long, the wake is quickly obliterated by the sea and leeway is likely to be greatest. However, after a number of passages in a yacht it is possible to build up a picture of the amount of leeway she makes under different conditions. With luck, the necessary information can be gained on relatively easy passages in good visibility so that it can be applied when it is most important, in bad visibility.

Leeway is applied, down wind, to the true course steered, to give wake course, the wake course being the direction in which the boat actually moves through the water. For example:

	Course steered	070°(T)	
	Estimated leeway	10°	wind from the north-west
	Wake course	080°(T)	(Fig 1.22)
or	Course steered	240°(T)	
	Estimated leeway	15°	wind from the north-west
	Wake course	225°(T)	

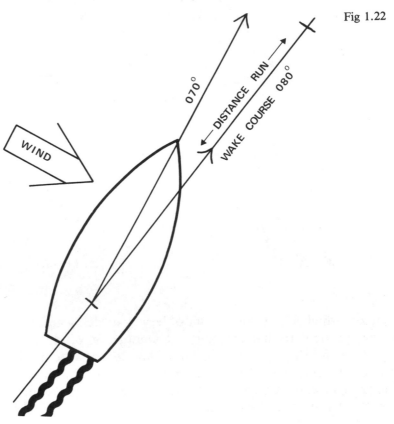

Fig 1.22

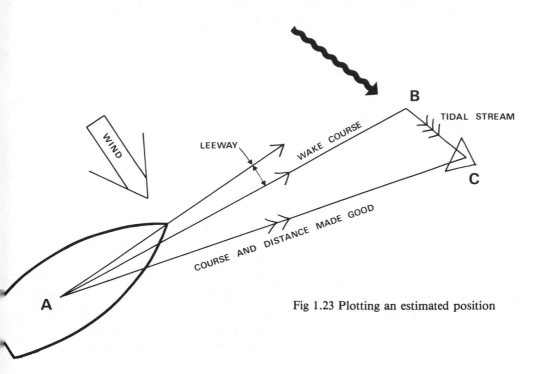

Fig 1.23 Plotting an estimated position

Plotting the Estimated Position

There is a simple routine for plotting estimated position:

1. Apply the estimated leeway to the true course steered to find the wake course.
2. From the last known position (A) lay off the direction of the wake course.
3. Along the wake course, measure the distance run by the log, having first applied any log error (AB).
4. Plot the set and drift of the tidal stream (BC).
5. Plot the estimated position at C.

Plot the course and distance made good (AC) (Fig 1.23).

If this procedure is applied to a numerical example it might give:

Course steered 040°(C), deviation 2°E, variation 9°W, estimated leeway 10° with wind from the north-west. Distance logged 5M. Tidal stream setting 120°(T), drift 1·5M.

Course steered	040°(C)
Deviation	2°E
Magnetic course	042°(M)
Variation	9°W
True course steered	033°(T)
Leeway to starboard	10°(down wind)
Wake course	043°(T)

The vectors can now be plotted to give the estimated position and course and distance made good (Fig 1.24, overleaf).

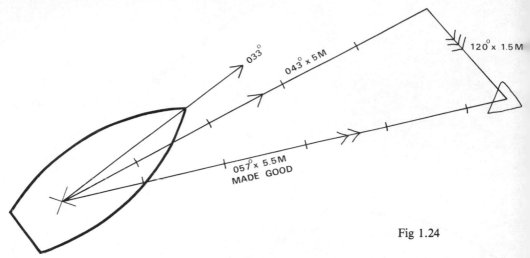

Fig 1.24

So far, we have considered a simple situation with the yacht on a steady course and the tidal stream constant in set and rate. More complex situations are illustrated in the three examples below and it will be seen that the principles involved are exactly the same as in the simple situation. The plotting of these three examples is shown in Fig 1.25 on page 40. In each case variation is 8°W and deviation as shown in the table on page 31.

Example 1.6
At 1000 a motor yacht is in position 50°00′.0N 4°50′.0W steering 340°(C) speed 6 knots. At 1024 course is altered to 020°(C) and speed is reduced to 5·5 knots. The tidal stream is slack between 1000 and 1100 and there is no wind. Plot the estimated position of the yacht at 1100. (As there is no tidal stream or leeway the estimated position will be the same as the dead-reckoning position.)

> Between 1000 and 1024:
> Course steered   340°(C)
> Compass error   0
> Course steered   340°(T)
> Distance run, 24 minutes at 6 knots
> $= 0·4 \times 6·0 = 2·4M$

From the 1000 position plot 340°(T) 2·4M.

> Between 1024 and 1100:
> Course steered   020°(C)
> Compass error   4°W
> Course steered   016°(T)
> Distance run, 36 minutes at 5·5 knots
> $= 0·6 \times 5·5 = 3·3M$

From the 1024 DR position plot 016°(T) 3·3M, which gives the 1100 DR (and in this case EP) position.

38

Example 1.7

At 1700 a yacht is in position 50°05′.6N 4°59′.3W, steering 060°(C), log reading 109·3. The wind is from the north, estimated leeway 6°.

At 1724 the yacht is hove to on port tack to reduce sail, log reading 111·4. At 1740 reefing is completed, the log reading is 111·9, the yacht having drifted in the estimated direction 120°(T) while hove to. The course steered from 1740 is 055°(C) and leeway is now estimated to be 4°. At 1800 the log reading is 113·5. The tidal stream between 1700 and 1800 has set 067°(T) at 2·3 knots. Plot the estimated position at 1800.

Between 1700 and 1724:

Course steered	060°(C)
Compass error	7°W
Course steered	053°(T)
Leeway (applied down wind)	6°
Wake course	059°(T)
Distance run = 111·4 − 109·3 = 2·1M	
Plot 059°(T) 2·1M	
Tidal stream set 067°(T) drift 0·9M	
(24 minutes at 2·3 knots)	

Plot tidal-stream vector to give 1724 EP.

Between 1724 and 1740:

Wake course	120°(T)
Distance run 0·5M	
Plot 120°(T) 0·5M	
Tidal stream set 067°(T) drift 0·6M	

Plot tidal-stream vector to give 1740 EP.

Between 1740 and 1800:

Course steered	055°(C)
Compass error	7°W
Course steered	048°(T)
Leeway (applied down wind)	4°
Wake course	052°(T)
Distance run by log 1·6M	
Plot 052°(T) 1·6M	
Tidal stream set 067°(T) drift 0·8M	

Plot tidal-stream vector to give 1800 EP.

(*Note*: The same result would have been obtained by plotting the three yacht's vectors and a single tidal-stream vector of 067°(T) 2·3M for the hour.)

39

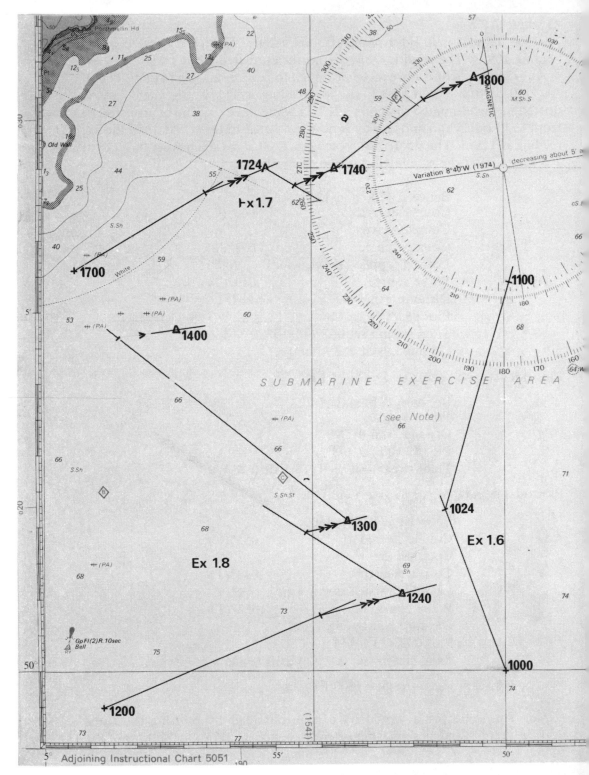

Fig 1.25 Examples of plotting estimated positions

Example 1.8

At 1200 a yacht is in position 49°59′.5N 4°58′.7W, log reading 54·2, steering 070°(C) close hauled on the port tack, making an estimated 5° leeway. At 1240, log reading 57·5, she tacks on to starboard to steer 310°(C), again making an estimated 5° leeway. Between 1200 and 1300 the tidal stream is setting 075°(T) at 1·8 knots. At 1300 the log reads 59·1 and between 1300 and 1400 the mean course steered is 315°(C), leeway 3°. At 1400 the log reads 63·2. Between 1300 and 1400 the tidal stream sets 082°(T) at 0·8 knots. Plot the EP at 1400.

Between 1200 and 1240:
Course steered	070°(C)
Compass error	8°W
Course steered	062°(T)
Leeway (applied down wind)	5°
Wake course	067°(T)
Distance run by log 3·3M	
Plot 067°(T) 3·3M	
Tidal stream set 075°(T) drift 1·2M	

Plot tidal-stream vector to give 1240 EP.

Between 1240 and 1300:
Course steered	310°(C)
Compass error	3°W
Course steered	307°(T)
Leeway (applied down wind)	5°
Wake course	302°(T)
Distance run by log 1·6M	
Plot 302°(T) 1·6M	
Tidal stream set 075°(T) drift 0·6M	

Plot tidal-stream vector to give 1300 EP.

Between 1300 and 1400:
Course steered	315°(C)
Compass error	3°W
Course steered	312°(T)
Leeway (applied down wind)	3°
Wake course	309°(T)
Distance run by log 4·1M	
Plot 309°(T) 4·1M	
Tidal stream set 082°(T) drift 0·8M	

Plot tidal-stream vector to give 1400 EP.

Finding a Course to Steer to Counteract Wind and Tidal Stream

Finding a course to steer to counteract wind and tidal stream involves the construction of a vector triangle and is therefore to some extent similar to plotting an EP. However, the order of working is completely different and it is most important not to confuse these two forms of plot.

Fig 1.26 Course to steer to counteract leeway and tidal stream

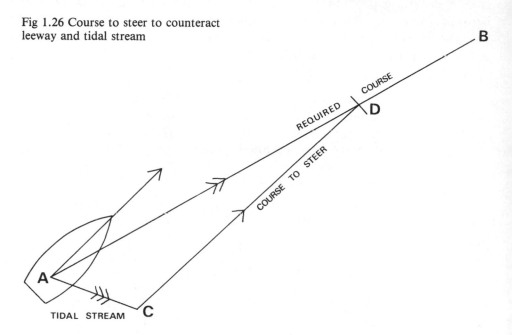

The order of working, illustrated in Fig 1.26, is as follows:

1 Lay off the required course on the chart from the starting position to the destination and label it with two arrows (AB). Here we are constructing half a vector, we know the direction, but as yet we do not know the speed we will make good.

2 Decide the time-scale for the vector triangle. It is normally convenient to construct a 1-hour triangle but there is no reason why a longer or shorter time should not be used.

3 Lay off the set and drift of the tidal stream from the starting position (AC) and label with three arrows.

4 From C strike off an arc on the required course a distance representing the distance run through the water in 1 hour to give point D. Draw the vector CD and label with one arrow.

5 The direction CD represents the wake course required. The distance AD represents the speed made good.

6 Apply the estimated angle of leeway *into the wind* to give the true course to steer.

Two common errors must be avoided. The first is to join the end of the tidal-stream vector (C) to the destination. If the destination happens to be exactly 1 hour's sailing away this will give the right answer, but under any other circumstances it will not. The second is to construct the wrong triangle, working out an EP on the assumption that the required course is steered, finding the angle between the resulting wake course and course made good and applying this angle up-tide. If the rate of the tidal stream is small this method gives approximately the right answer, but with a fast tidal stream it gives a completely wrong answer.

A numerical example of the correct procedure is illustrated in Fig 1.27. The direction from the starting position to the destination is 060°(T), distance 8M. The tidal stream is setting 110°(T) at 1·6 knots. The speed of the yacht is 5 knots.

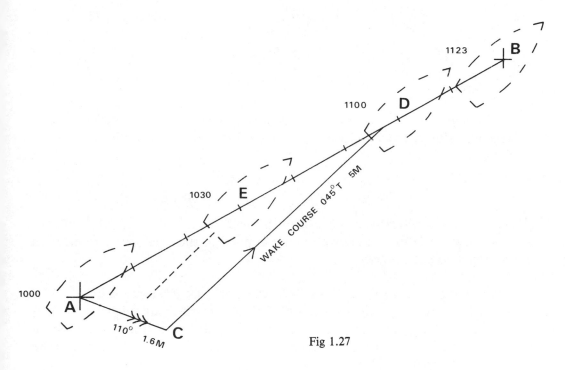

Fig 1.27

The order of working is:

1   Plot AB, the direction to be made good.
2   Plot AC, the tidal set and drift for 1 hour.
3   Strike off an arc of radius 5 miles from C to give the position D.
4   Join CD.

Note that ACD is a construction to find the direction CD, the wake course required. The yacht moves along AB, reaching position E after ½ hour and D after 1 hour, making good a speed of 5·8 knots, represented by the distance AD. She will reach her destination, B, after 1 hour 23 minutes.

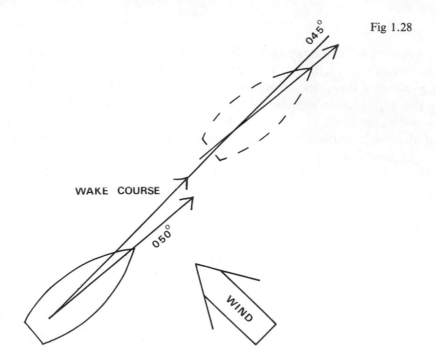

Fig 1.28

The estimated leeway is applied to the wake course, into the wind. In our example above, assuming leeway of 5° with a south-east wind:

Wake course required	045°(T)
Leeway (applied into wind)	5°
Course to steer	050°(T)

The situation described is illustrated in Fig 1.28.

Finally, variation and deviation are applied to the true course to give the compass course to steer.

Finding a Course to Counteract Tidal Stream Over a Short Period

Fig 1.29 shows a yacht in position 200°(T) Lizard Point Lighthouse 3M, bound for Penzance. The course required to clear the Boa overfalls by a good margin is 310°(T). The tidal stream is setting 067° at 2·3 knots and the estimated leeway is 6° in a south-west wind. Speed is 5 knots.

The vector triangle shows that the wake course required is 286°(T), with a speed made good of 3·5 knots.

Wake course required	286°(T)
Leeway (applied into wind)	6°
Course to steer	280°(T)
Variation	8°W
Magnetic course	288°(M)
Deviation	2°E
Compass course to steer	286°(C)

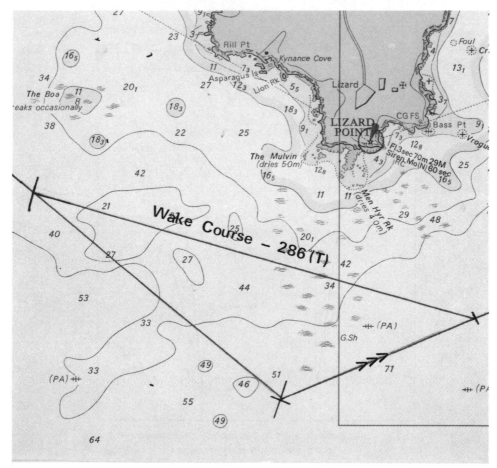

Fig 1.29

Finding the Course to Counteract Tidal Stream Over a Long Passage
To find the course to steer over a long passage, say, across the English
Channel, it is first necessary to calculate approximately how long the passage
will take and then find the tidal-stream set and drift for the duration of the
passage. If the tidal streams are more or less rectilinear, that is to say, flow
only in two opposing directions, to find the excess drift in one direction is a
very simple calculation. However, if the tidal streams are rotary, that is to
say, the direction changes from hour to hour, it will be necessary to plot the
vectors of set and drift for each hour to find the resultant for the total
duration of the passage. Both methods are illustrated overleaf in Fig 1.30.

Finding a single course to steer throughout a passage instead of working
out a new course to steer each hour as the stream changes reduces the amount
of chart-work and also cuts down the time taken on passage. The accuracy of
the course found depends upon the correct assessment of the speed at which
the passage will be made, which is easier to achieve under power than under
sail. Steering a single course across the flood and ebb of a tidal cycle may

45

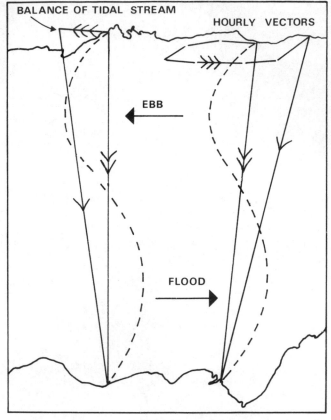

BALANCE OF TIDAL STREAM

HOURLY VECTORS

EBB

FLOOD

Fig 1.30 Course to steer to counteract tidal stream, with
rectilinear and rotary streams

take the yacht a long way from the rhumb line, so it is important to check
that there are no adjacent dangers.

Let us consider an example of a Channel crossing. A motor yacht on
passage from Fowey to Roscoff sets course from position 50°07′N 4°33′W.
The distance to the destination is 84M and the expected speed 7 knots, so the
passage time will be 12 hours. The tidal-stream predictions for the passage
are:

Hours	Set	Rate
1	080°	0·9
2	080°	1·4
3	080°	1·2
4	080°	0·6
5	080°	0·2
6	Slack	
7	260°	1·4
8	260°	1·7
9	260°	1·4

10		Slack
11	080°	1·7
12	080°	3·1

Total drift 080° 9·1M
Total drift 260° 4·5M
Balance   080° 4·6M

The method of plotting is:

1 Plot the balance of the tidal stream from the initial position.
2 Strike off the distance through the water against the required track to find the true course to steer.
3 Apply leeway, variation and deviation.

2 Navigational Instruments

A recent survey of the British chandlery business revealed that almost 50 per cent of the money spent in chandlers' shops was for electric and electronic equipment — clear proof, if any were needed, of the bewildering array of 'magic boxes' which are available. Some of the wizardry — radio-telephones, for example — is not really navigational equipment, but most comes under that heading. The very complexity of the available equipment tends to mask the fact that the basic needs of the navigator for navigational instruments are simple but that the basic ones must be absolutely reliable.

Presentation of Information

All navigational instruments present information, by illuminated digit or by analogue (some form of pointer on a dial), and it is important to appreciate the advantages and disadvantages of the different forms of presentation. Analogue presentation can be read without the navigator actually having to read anything — the brain merely absorbs an impression of the position of a pointer. No great accuracy is achieved but a helmsman can look at a compass card and, with little effort, see that the heading is, say, just to port of 310°(C). The brain never actually registers the heading of the boat as a number of degrees; the helm is moved so that the boat returns to her required course. This process would require much more thought and concentration if the steering compass had a digital display. If the required course was 310°(C) it would require considerable mental effort to interpret the action required when the compass display read 307°(C). On the other hand, when great accuracy is important a digital presentation — of speed for sail trimming, for example — can present a clear difference between 5·3 knots and 5·4 knots in a manner which would be almost impossible with a small pointer on the dial of a meter.

By any standards, the steering compass is the most important navigational instrument in a yacht. Other instruments which are normally fitted — all of more or less equal importance — are the log, hand-bearing compass, echo-sounder and radio direction-finder. Less essential for purely navigational purposes are wind speed and direction indicators and, in an altogether different class of expense, are sophisticated radio position-fixing systems such as Decca Navigator, Loran C, Omega and satellite navigator.

Planning and Installation

More disappointments and frustration are caused in small craft by lack of thought in planning and installation than by defects in the instruments themselves. The worst way to install any equipment is to buy it on impulse and then wander around the cockpit or navigating area wondering where to put it.

As with sailing clothes, sleeping arrangements or cooking, the golden rule is 'Think rough'. In good weather almost anything will serve; it is only in bad conditions that the advantages of intelligent pre-planning really prove themselves.

There can be few other hard and fast rules on the installation of navigational instruments, but a number of considerations will narrow down the choice of available sites. Is it vulnerable? Is it hermetically sealed or merely splash-proof? Is it itself highly magnetic or does it contain a compass and need to be sited clear of other magnetic influences? Does the helmsman need to see it easily from his normal steering position? Are repeaters available which would provide more convenient presentation? Is it likely to be referred to continuously or only on rare occasions? Does it need constant adjustment?

Ideally, all the navigational instruments should be fitted at the same time so that there is a logical system about the way they are sited. This is not too difficult to plan. The real problem arises when a new instrument is added to the outfit.

Chart Tables

The position and size of the chart table itself is likely to be decided by the designer of the yacht rather than by the owner. Some owners, however, have the opportunity to specify the size of table, while others may be able to fit a makeshift one themselves. To spread a full size Admiralty chart requires an area 106cm × 71cm (42in × 28in) and, unless the chart table doubles as the saloon table, this amount of space is usually only found in large yachts. It is certainly convenient to be able to use an unfolded chart, but the size of the chart table must be decided in relation to the rest of the available space. It is probably more convenient to have a half-size chart table and accept the necessity to fold charts than to share the table with every meal served on board.

The 'Think rough' rule applies also to chart tables. In heavy weather the navigator is bound to have to brace himself against the table so ensure that it is strong. It is easier to work on a chart on the cabin sole than on a flimsy plywood board held in place by two small screws and a dab of glue.

Lighting

The lighting on the chart table and navigational instruments is important. Even on a dark night it is usually possible for the crew to do almost everything that has to be done on deck without resorting to torches or deck lights if the instruments are carefully lit and there is absolutely no stray light from below. Once a single bright light is used the crew's night vision (their ability to see in almost total darkness) is destroyed. Ideally, the whole accommodation should be lit with a number of very low-powered lights. The resulting glow should be sufficient to enable the crew to go below for another sweater without having to use a bright light. The chart table light should give the navigator just enough light to see the chart; it should be fitted with a dimmer and carefully screened to prevent scatter. The instrument lighting can then be very dim and it is only necessary to illuminate a part of some of the instruments, for instance, the few degrees of the compass card either side of the heading marker.

Until very recently it was believed that red light did not impair night vision, whereas white light did. Recent research has shown, however, that it is not so much the colour of a light but its brightness which is important. A red shade is likely to reduce the intensity of a light by about 80 per cent, so it is an effective means of reducing brightness.

Steering Compasses

A steering compass should be sited so that it is clearly visible to the helmsman, is as far as possible from ferrous metal and electrical equipment which will give rise to large deviations, and is not vulnerable to damage. There are three broad types of compass: the flat-topped, dome-topped and edge-reading.

The flat-topped type must be mounted in gimbals. The card itself has limited freedom to rotate about its horizontal axes, so unless the whole compass is gimballed the card comes into contact with the top of the compass as soon as the boat heels and is unable to align itself with the magnetic meridian.

This type of instrument is frequently fitted with a grid, a reference line on the top glass which can be set to the required course. The helmsman aligns a graduation on the card itself with the graduation on the top glass to maintain course. The steering grid is much easier to interpret at a glance than the compass card itself, so minimal concentration is required to steer.

The grid compass suffers from two disadvantages. The first is that because it is flat-topped, it must be viewed from above so the helmsman is looking in the general direction of the cockpit sole each time he looks at the compass. Most people steer by a combination of looking at the compass, the bow of the boat swinging against the background of the horizon and, in sailing boats, the set of the sails. Thus, a compass which is mounted close to the helmsman's line of sight to the horizon allows him to watch two of his reference points with the minimum of difficulty, and by the nature of its construction this cannot be achieved with a grid compass. The second disadvantage is that the helmsman never actually steers a course in terms of a number of degrees; rather, he aligns two reference marks. Frequently the helmsman will be unable to maintain the required course and, if he is using a grid compass, he may be unable to tell at the end of his trick what his mean course steered has actually been, information which is important to the navigator in working out his EP.

The dome-topped card-reading compass is easily read at an oblique angle and may not require to be gimballed if the card is free to rotate about the horizontal axes. It is therefore easier to site and, if it is not gimballed, less vulnerable to damage by heavy-footed crew members than a flat-topped compass.

The edge-reading compass is growing in popularity. A number of versions are now available which are suitable for mounting on the bulkhead at the forward end of the cockpit. In a sailing boat a highly satisfactory steering-compass system consists of two edge-reading instruments, one on each side of the cockpit. With this system the helmsman has a compass close to his natural line of sight forwards, whichever side of the cockpit he sits.

The traditional steering compass is read at the forward end of the card, the lubber's mark used for heading reference being at the forward side of the compass bowl. With an edge-reading compass the heading reference is at the back of the instrument, so the whole process of steering by the compass appears to be reversed. This is not a problem to anyone accustomed to an edge-reading instrument, but many people are confused when they have to change from one type to another.

In a yacht built of steel or with a large amount of ferrous metal in her construction, it may be impossible to site a steering compass where it can be seen by the helmsman without its being badly affected by the magnetic influence of the hull. In such cases the answer is a transmitting compass, with the sensing unit sited away from magnetic influences, possibly up a mast, and a repeater unit mounted in a convenient position for the helmsman.

Hand-bearing Compasses

The hand-bearing compass is used to take bearings of shore marks and other ships. The older compasses tend to be large, heavy and vulnerable to impact damage. Modern designs are available for compasses which can be carried on a lanyard around the neck and which are much more robust than the older models. There is little difference between the accuracy obtainable with the old and new types and many of the small modern instruments have optics arranged to eliminate parallax errors, thus making them that much simpler to use.

Taking accurate bearings with a hand-bearing compass requires practice. The commonest mistake made by beginners is to rush the operation. The card takes several seconds (often 10—15) to steady and if sufficient time is not allowed for it to do so, inaccurate bearings will result. It is also important to make sure that the compass is not held close to any ferrous metal or electrical equipment when a bearing is being taken.

Compass Swinging and Adjustment

In all yachts there is equipment containing ferrous metal which will cause deviation of the steering compass. In some cases, by judicious siting, it may be possible to reduce the deviation to a negligible amount; in others, particularly with steel or composite hulls, considerable deviation will be present, wherever the compass is sited. The deviation of the steering compass should be checked on the following occasions: on first commissioning a new boat; on resiting the compass; after any major structural work has been carried out; at the start of each sailing season. Whether or not it is necessary to place corrector magnets to reduce deviation depends upon the result of the deviation check. If deviation is found to be less than 2° on all headings it is not worth correcting the compass.

There are a number of methods of checking the compass for deviation, known as swinging the compass. They vary in complexity and the most suitable method depends on the siting of the compass and the geography of the area in which the swing is to be carried out.

Swing by Compass Comparison

The simplest method of checking the compass is to compare the heading by the steering compass with the heading by hand-bearing compass. If the boat is magnetically simple, which means that she has no galvanised rigging, guard-rails or stanchions and there are no integral structures such as frames of iron or steel, acceptable accuracy can be obtained by sighting along the centre-line with the hand-bearing compass from a position close to the back-stay. In a magnetically complicated boat it may be impossible to find a position on deck which is free from the boat's magnetic influence where the hand-bearing compass can be used. In this case, an observer with a hand-bearing compass can be towed astern in a dinghy, having first checked that the dinghy itself has no large ferrous metal components. It is possible to use this method only in calm conditions.

Whichever method is used to find ship's head with the hand-bearing compass the procedure is the same. The yacht is steadied on a cardinal point and the steering compass and hand-bearing compass headings compared. This is then repeated, approximately every 22½° around the compass, and a deviation table drawn up on the assumption that the hand-bearing compass has indicated magnetic bearings. Thus, the usefulness of the method depends upon the success which has been achieved in selecting a position to use the hand-bearing compass where it is not affected by the yacht's magnetic influence. A useful check on the validity of the deviations found can be made by plotting the graph of deviation against compass heading. The result should show a reasonably smooth curve, balanced about the zero axis.

Compass Swing by Transits or Bearings

An alternative method of checking the compass, which is independent of any other form of magnetic compass and hence more reliable, involves comparison of compass bearings with the chartered bearings of transits. The ideal location is a beacon in the centre of a bay or estuary. The beacon is used as the front mark and aligned with more distant objects, with the fore and aft line of the yacht also aligned with the transit. It will never be possible to find marks which provide sixteen natural transits equally spaced at 22½° intervals, but it is often possible to find ten or twelve usefully situated marks which allow the deviation to be determined at intervals around the 360°. Again, deviation should be plotted against compass heading and as long as a reasonably smooth curve results, the intermediate deviations can be deduced from the curve.

If the yacht's position can be determined accurately and the reference marks used are distant, a variation of this method can be used without any front transit mark. An acceptable degree of accuracy (±1°) is obtained if the boat's position is known to 100m and the reference mark is at least 3 miles away. Instead of comparing the compass bearing with a chartered bearing of a transit, the compass heading is compared with the chartered bearing of the distant object from the known position of the yacht.

Other methods of swinging the compass depend on the ability to take bearings with the steering compass. This is only possible with very few types of steering compass or with the use of a pelorus, an azimuth ring which is mounted on deck and aligned manually with the steering compass.

Heeling Error

One type of deviation, known as heeling error, may not be detected by the type of swing described above. Heeling error is caused by a vertical component of the yacht's magnetic field and it varies in proportion to the angle of heel, from zero when upright, increasing as the heel increases. Its presence can be detected by measuring the deviation with the boat upright and heeled on a number of headings, but it is not realistic to make any allowance for it. It must be corrected, therefore, by placing compensating magnets under the compass.

In general the correction of a compass is best left to an expert as it requires special equipment. Placing the necessary corrector magnets is sometimes a simple matter, but the amateur can go wrong and overcorrect his compass to the extent that it becomes useless as a heading reference.

Logs and Speedometers

As with most navigational instruments, the choice of logs and speedometers is bewilderingly large.

Towed Logs

The simplest form of log consists of a rotor which drives some form of mechanical counting device. The rotor works like a propeller in reverse — the faster the yacht travels through the water the faster it rotates.

The best known of the simple mechanical logs is the Walker, in which the rotor is trailed astern on a length of log-line and the counting mechanism and display are mounted on the taffrail. The main virtue of the Walker log is its simplicity and, for this reason, it is popular with long-distance yachtsmen. One of its drawbacks is that if the yacht goes astern with the log streamed, the line is likely to become entangled in the propeller.

Streaming and handing a towed log require a certain amount of skill to avoid putting kinks in the line. Streaming it, the line should be clipped to its hook on the back of the display, the bight of the line streamed and then the rotor thrown clear. Handing it, the line should be unclipped and the inboard end paid out quickly around a stanchion as the rotor is recovered. Then the line can be coiled from the rotor end.

Hull-mounted Logs

More complex mechanical logs use a rotor mounted under the hull with a flexible wire drive to the display. This eliminates the need to stream and hand the log, but the rotor is much less accessible if it is fouled by a lump of weed or a polythene bag.

The more sophisticated versions of the rotor type of log dispense with the mechanical link between rotor and display. The rotor actuates an electric or electronic counter to measure speed and distance, which are displayed at a convenient location at the chart table or in the cockpit. The advantage of using an electrical system instead of a mechanical one is that a considerably less powerful, and hence much smaller, rotor can be used. Some sacrifice in simplicity is inevitable as soon as an electrical mechanism is used, but this must be balanced against the much lower drag of a smaller rotor.

All logs which use an underwater rotating mechanism are liable to fouling problems by weed, polythene bags and other floating debris. Most rotors are of the propeller type, but some work on the paddle-wheel principle, with only the lower padddles projecting beneath the hull. The paddle-wheel type is much less vulnerable to fouling than the propeller variety, but also generally less accurate.

Logs are also available which measure speed and distance without using any moving parts. These are activated either by the pressure of the water moving past the hull or by an electro-magnetic or electronic principle. They have the advantage of greater freedom from fouling, but tend to be sensitive to siting problems as they have exacting requirements for freedom from areas of turbulent water flow if they are to give accurate results.

Most logs give a direct reading of both distance run and speed through the water. The more sophisticated also have a facility to provide an expanded speed-scale so that an increase or decrease in speed of 0·1 knot is immediately apparent. This type of display is particularly useful in a racing boat as it shows the effect on speed of a small adjustment to the trim or set of the sails.

Highly sophisticated is the log which uses twin rotors, one on each side of the hull with a gravity change-over switch so that the more deeply immersed rotor is always in use. This type of fitting has the added advantage that if one rotor is fouled the gravity switch can be overridden manually and the clear rotor used until the obstruction has been removed.

Log Errors

No log is likely to give absolute accuracy. Every log attempts to measure distance and speed *through the water*. Any movement of the water itself in the vicinity of the rotor-sensing mechanism will not be registered by the log and, as the sensing mechanism is invariably close to the surface, an apparent error may be induced by surface drift in prolonged strong winds. There is a minimum speed, usually between 1 and 2 knots, below which only the best logs will register accurately. This is relatively unimportant because distance is covered so slowly at very low speeds that, even if the log ceases to register completely, the total error in position builds up very slowly.

In general, the inaccuracies to which logs are susceptible are caused by one or both of two reasons. Every log has in-built inaccuracies, albeit very small ones in the better instruments; however carefully the rotor or sensor is sited, it is likely to be subject to some turbulence which induces false readings. The first of these inaccuracies is likely to be a reasonably constant percentage of speed; the second is less so, as sea conditions have a marked effect.

Log Calibration

It is possible to determine the inaccuracy of the log by runs over a measured distance. The results, strictly speaking, are valid only for the particular sea conditions prevailing at the time.

Unless an area free of tidal streams can be found, two runs over the measured distance are required. For very accurate results, except where the tidal stream is constant in rate, four runs should be made. The measured distance may be either purpose made, with a set of transit beacons at each end, or it may simply be the charted distance between two points. In either case, the course steered during the runs should always be along the charted direction of the distance, with no allowance made for cross component of tidal stream.

The elapsed time for each run is measured by a stop-watch and the speed by log recorded at intervals of, say, 15 seconds so that the mean speed by log for the run can be deduced. The percentage error of the log is then calculated using the formula:

$$C = 100 \frac{S_1 + S_2}{L_1 + L_2} - 1$$

where: C is percentage log correction

S$_1$ and S$_2$ are the calculated speed over the ground for runs one and two

L$_1$ and L$_2$ are the mean speed by the log for runs one and two.

For example:

A yacht makes two runs over a measured distance of 1 sea mile.
On the first run the time taken is 12 minutes 48 seconds and the mean speed by log is 4·73 knots.
On the second run the time taken is 11 minutes 30 seconds and the mean speed by log is 4·81 knots.

On the first run, speed over the ground is:

$$1 \times \frac{60}{12 \cdot 8} = 4 \cdot 69 \text{ knots}$$

On the second run, speed over the ground is:

$$1 \times \frac{60}{11 \cdot 5} = 5 \cdot 22 \text{ knots}$$

Applying the formula:

$$C = 100 \frac{4 \cdot 69 + 5 \cdot 22}{4 \cdot 73 + 4 \cdot 81} - 1$$

$$= +4 \text{ per cent.}$$

This is the percentage error to apply to the log reading, for speed or distance, to give the true speed or distance through the water.

It is easier to use the speed rather than distance recorded by the log to find the percentage error because a more accurate reading of speed can be obtained. On most logs the distance recorded changes only every tenth of a mile, so the recorded distance over a measured mile could be in error by as much as 10 per cent because of the coarseness of the distance recording mechanism rather than because of any actual inaccuracy. Any discrepancy between speed and distance recorded by the log can be detected by noting the time taken and mean speed recorded to cover exactly 1 mile by the log. The

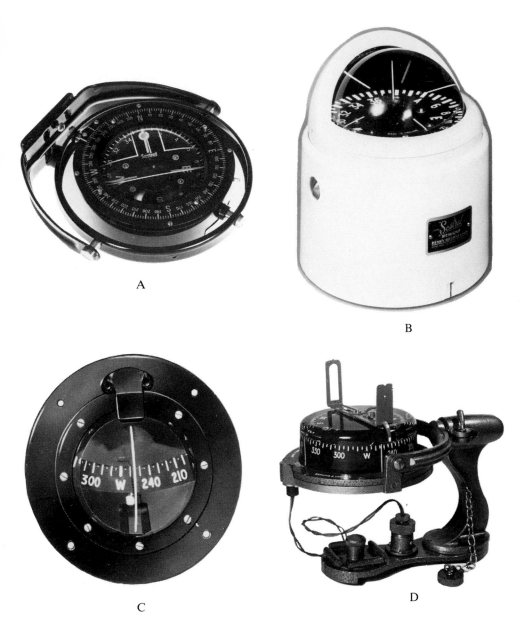

Fig 2.1 STEERING COMPASSES

A A flat-topped grid compass. Note gimbals
B A dome-topped steering compass. The card is free to align itself with the horizontal so exterior gimbals are not required
C An edge-reading compass for bulkhead mountings
D A Sestrel Moore compass, normally fitted as an edge-reading steering compass, with the added facility of a bearing sight
(photographs courtesy of Henry Browne & Son Ltd)

A

B

Fig 2.2 HAND-BEARING COMPASS
A   The traditional style of hand-bearing compass on the left has a bowl 108mm in diameter,
     an overall height of 215mm and a weight of 1.30Kg
B   The more compact modern style on the right is 84mm × 36mm and weighs just 0.16Kg
     (photographs courtesy of Offshore Instruments Ltd and Henry Browne & Son Ltd)

A

B

C

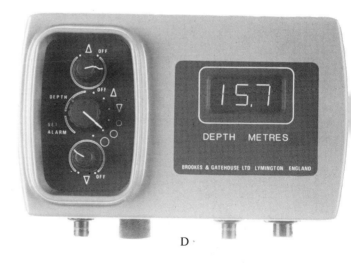

D

Fig 2.3 TYPICAL ECHO-SOUNDER DISPLAYS

A   A simple rotating-light model
B   A more sophisticated model, incorporating variable power output, three range scales and
    an alarm which gives audible warning at a pre-set depth
C   A remote display for a needle-and-pointer sounder
D   A digital-reading sounder, also incorporating an audible alarm
    (photographs courtesy of Electronic Laboratories Ltd and Brooks & Gatehouse Ltd)

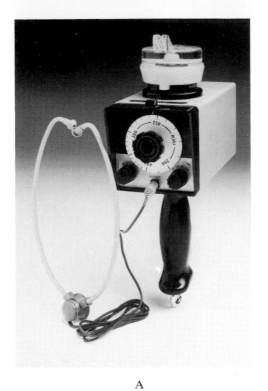

A

B

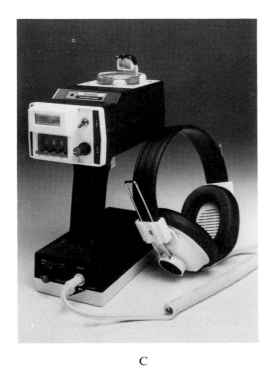

C

D

Fig 2.4 RADIO DIRECTION-FINDERS
A   A very simple dial-tuned set, with the compass mounted on the receiver
B   A more sophisticated model, with the aerial and compass in a separate unit
C & D   Digital-tuned receivers

run is started and ended at an exact point in the distance-recorder cycle, so the coarseness of the record is unimportant.

If meticulous navigational records are kept, it is possible to build up a detailed estimate of the accuracy of the log over a range of different sea conditions and it should be the aim of every yacht owner or navigator to do this.

Echo-sounders

Again there is a bewilderingly large choice of echo-sounders available but the principle on which they all operate is the same: a pulse of sound is transmitted through a transducer on the bottom of the boat and the time interval until reception of the returning echo from the sea bed is measured. As the velocity of sound in water is, for all practical purposes, constant, the time interval can be displayed as a depth.

The choice comes in the method of display. The four basic types of display are rotating light (either neon or LED); dial and pointer; digital; and paper recording.

The rotating-light display gives a flash at zero as the transmission occurs and a second flash at the indicated depth. In shallow water there may be an additional flash at twice the actual depth caused by a 'double bounce' echo. On most sets two depth scales are available, the deeper usually being six times the shallower, a legacy from the days when the fathom was the primary unit of depth. Most sounders of this type tend to be unsophisticated. Some of them are difficult to read in bright light, although this defect is being over-come by modern display techniques. Because the display incorporates a relatively large rotating mechanism, power consumption is relatively high and of course the bearings of the rotating assembly are subject to wear. The display is also capable of recording a depth beyond the nominal limit of the scale, which can be a disturbing feature. If the maximum scale depth is, say, 20m, and the depth of water is, say, 25m, this is displayed as 5m. Switching to a deeper range scale, if one is available, reveals the true depth and, because of the limited power output, second trace recordings rarely register on the deep scale.

Dial and pointer displays are usually associated with more expensive and sophisticated sounders. They overcome the difficulty of 'blacking' in bright light and the needle is much lighter and slower moving than a continuously rotating assembly, which gives the needle system advantages in terms of power consumption and mechanical wear.

Digital display is a further option which has recently become available. The clarity and precision of this type of display are obvious advantages and the power required is minimal.

The paper-recording type of display has considerable advantages for fishing and survey work, but it has no particular advantages over other displays for cruising or yacht-racing. The need to keep it supplied with recording paper is an unwarranted nuisance.

Depth Alarms

Many echo-sounders provide an alarm facility. The alarm can be pre-set to sound a buzzer at one or more pre-determined depths. The obvious use is to set the alarm to give warning of shoaling water. It is also particularly useful when short tacking along a depth-contour line to set one alarm to sound at a minimum depth and the other at a maximum depth. Without the alarm facility it might be necessary to have a member of the crew permanently watching the sounder.

Errors of Echo-sounders

Most echo-sounders fitted in yachts operate on the assumption that the velocity of sound in sea water is constant. This is not quite true since it varies slightly with temperature and salinity. Any inaccuracy caused by these variations, however, is likely to be small and certainly negligible in depths of less then 5m.

The simplest sounders record depth below the transducer, which is not the same thing as depth below the keel or depth below the surface. More sophisticated models can be adjusted to read either depth below the surface or below the keel and it is important to know what setting has been applied. By convention, the sounder should be set to read depth below the surface as this makes tidal reduction calculations slightly easier.

All sounders convert an elapsed time to a depth. The method of doing so varies, but in most it depends upon a fixed-value power supply. The wrong power supply therefore gives an inaccurate reading and a low supply is particularly dangerous as it tends to give rise to a false reading deeper than the actual. Some sounders incorporate a battery-check function, which should be used whenever the instrument is switched on and at intervals while it is in use.

Nomenclature of Changes of Depth

Confusion can arise in talking about changes of depth. If one member of the crew is watching the sounder and reporting depths, he should use the verbs 'deepening' or 'shoaling' to indicate changes. These are unambiguous terms about which there can be no confusion. The use of the words 'rising' or 'falling' in relation to change of depth should be avoided as they might refer to the height of the sea bed or the numbers on the echo-sounder.

Lead Lines

The lead line is the traditional sounding device and although many now regard it as obsolete, it has a number of advantages over the electronic echo-sounder. It is more or less impervious to damp, does not require an electrical power supply and is very cheap. It can also give a good indication, by picking up samples in a blob of tallow or grease in the recess of the base, of the nature of the sea bed. This is a particularly useful feature when searching for a patch of sand or mud to anchor.

There is a recognised conventional code of symbols for marking a lead line, but any system of knots, pieces of string with knots or strips of distinctive material will serve. The conventional code is:

1, 11 and 21m — one strip of leather
2, 12 and 22m — two strips of leather
3, 13 and 23m — blue bunting
4, 14 and 24m — green and white bunting
5, 15 and 25m — white bunting
6, 16 and 26m — green bunting
7, 17 and 27m — red bunting
8, 18 and 28m — blue and white bunting
9, 19 and 29m — red and white bunting
10m — leather with a hole in it
20m — leather with a hole in it and 2 strips of leather

Radio Direction-finders

Radio direction-finding is, to most yachtsmen, the primary source of positional information when out of sight of land. There is an established network of MF radio beacons around our coasts. These marine radio-beacons are supplemented by air radio-beacons, which, although intended primarily for aeronautical use, can also be used for marine navigation.

Marine radio-beacons are arranged in groups, with up to six beacons sharing a single frequency. They transmit in sequence over a 6-minute period, so each beacon transmits for 1 minute. A typical transmission consists of a morse identification signal, a long continuous transmission and a final morse identification. It is possible to identify a beacon either by its morse identification signal or by its time of transmission and frequency. Full details of groupings, frequencies and identification signals appear in the *Admiralty List of Radio Signals*, Volume II, and slightly abbreviated details in yachtsmen's nautical almanacs.

The method of identification of a beacon depends upon the type of transmission and the type of receiver used. This is a slightly complicated subject. Two modes of emission are used: the morse signal in one is produced by keying the carrier wave (designated A2 in *ALRS*); in the other the carrier wave is transmitted continuously throughout the 1 minute the beacon is in use, and the morse signal is produced by keying a superimposed tone (designated A2*). If a receiver incorporating a beat frequency oscillator

(BFO) is used, it may not be possible to detect the superimposed tone and hence the morse identification signal. In such cases, the best means of identifying a beacon is by its frequency and transmission time.

Direction finding is possible either with a special DF receiver or with a direction-finding aerial used in conjunction with a receiver which can be tuned to the required part of the MF band. Modern designs of DF receiver include extremely efficient digital tuned receivers, in which the required frequency is entered by a keyboard. This allows very accurate tuning which is not possible with the traditional rotating scale tuning system. Digital tuned receivers may also incorporate a quartz digital clock for beacon sequence identification.

Direction-finding Aerials

Direction-finding aerials are either hand-held, incorporating a compass very similar to a hand-bearing compass, rotating loop, with an azimuth ring graduated relative to ship's head, or fixed loop, in which the reception from the loops is electrically rotated against an azimuth ring graduated relative to ship's head.

The hand-held aerial gives a magnetic bearing of the beacon. This has the obvious advantage that it does not require the conversion of a relative bearing to a magnetic bearing before plotting, with the consequent reliance upon the helmsman steering an absolutely steady course while the bearing is being taken. Using an independent compass for radio bearings, however, does place constraints upon the positions in which the aerial can be used in order to avoid the deviating effect of the yacht's structure and fittings. The advantages and disadvantages of loop aerials are the converse of those of hand-held aerials.

Taking a Radio Bearing

The method of taking a radio bearing, once a beacon has been identified, is to find the null point, the direction of minimum signal. This is seldom absolutely clearly defined, and must be taken as the centre of a fade area — anything up to 30° in extent. The limits of the fade area can be defined by rotating the aerial in one direction until the signal fades, crossing the fade area and then returning to it to find the other side. It may appear possible to simplify the procedure by identifying one cut-off point as the signal fades and the other as it is regained. This simplification is not recommended, as the audio level at which a signal is lost may not be quite the same as the level at which it is gained.

Some direction-finding receivers incorporate a visual null meter to give a visual indication of null point. The value of such a meter is questionable as it is extremely difficult for the operator to watch both the indicated bearing and the null meter at the same time. Automatic direction-finders are also available which give a direct visual presentation of the bearing of the radio beacon.

There are in fact two nulls, one on the bearing of the station, the other on the reciprocal. Common sense will usually indicate which is the actual bearing to plot.

The accuracy achievable in a radio bearing depends largely upon the individual navigator's skill and experience. There are also a number of properties of radio waves which can give rise to errors:

Range: Signal strength and hence sharpness of null is directly related to range. At extreme ranges, particularly at night, the received signal may combine an element of sky-wave, which reduces the accuracy of the bearing.

Coastal Refraction: If the direct line between transmitter and receiver crosses the coast at an oblique angle, the radio waves may be refracted. Similarly, high land between transmitter and receiver may 'bend' the path of the radio waves. Most marine radio-beacons are situated on the coast to avoid refraction errors, but air beacons are often sited well inland and bearings on them are subject to refraction errors.

Dawn and Dusk Effect: For a period of about 1 hour around sunset and sunrise radio propagation is subject to anomalies. Bearings taken at those times are therefore unreliable.

Quadrantal Error: This might be considered as 'radio deviation'. It is caused by reflection of incoming signals by the yacht's structure and varies with the relative bearing of the beacon. It can be checked on any beacon which is visible by comparing the visual bearing with the radio bearing. With an aerial in a fixed position quadrantal errors can be tabulated against relative bearing, but with a hand-held aerial it is only possible to find a position in the boat which appears to give reasonably error-free results.

Clocks and Watches

Modern wrist watches are so accurate that a ship's clock is rapidly becoming an anachronism. It is important, however, that everyone involved in the navigation of a yacht should be using the same time base, and the easiest way to make sure this happens is to have a clock at the chart table or on a cabin bulkhead.

An accurate clock or watch can be extremely useful when using the radio direction-finder, to identify beacons from their time of transmission.

A stop-watch, or at least a watch with a second hand, is useful for identifying the characteristics of a light or fog signal.

Other Instruments

There is much which could be classified as navigational equipment and a great many sophisticated gadgets which have not been mentioned.

Electronic calculators of varying degrees of sophistication are used by many navigators. For coastal navigation they can be used instead of a pencil and a sheet of paper and they can give quick answers to simple mathematical calculations. However they do not allow the navigator to do anything which he could not do without a calculator. For someone who uses a calculator every day, it is logical to use one for navigation, but unless the navigator is practised in using a calculator, it is probably safer for him to stick to pencil and paper.

Sophisticated electronic fixing aids such as Decca, Omega, Loran C and satellite navigators are all available to the yachtsman with a deep pocket and a reliable power supply. All of these aids make it easier to establish the position of a yacht when she is out of sight of land, but none of them is essential for safe navigation

Radar is another aid to navigation. It is particularly useful because in restricted visibility it gives both an indication of other vessels in the vicinity and position-fixing ability. The disadvantages of radar are that the weight, size and siting requirements of the aerial make it unacceptable to some owners and, to a greater extent than with any other aid, its misuse can lead to dangers even greater than its proper use avoids.

The picture on a radar screen looks like the answer to every navigator's prayer so there is a tendency to orientate to the radar screen and forget about navigation. Chart-work seems unnecessary, but just as the land slips below the visible horizon so it fades from the radar screen. The position of every ship within 10 miles is clearly displayed, but the radar does not show their course, speed or aspect so it does not provide a direct answer to collision-avoidance problems. The fact that radar makes navigation in bad visibility possible means that it is an extremely useful aid, but it requires special techniques and a knowledge of its capabilities and limitations which are beyond the scope of this book.

3 Lights, Buoys and Pilotage

Lights

Lights to aid navigation are shown from lighthouses, lightvessels, buoys and beacons. The position of a lighthouse or a beacon is shown on the chart by a star. The exact position of a lightvessel or a buoy is indicated on the chart by a small circle at the base of the symbol. In all cases attention is drawn to the light by a magenta-coloured 'flash' on the chart.

Description of a Light

The description of a light is given on the chart in a standard order:

1 Characteristic: the distinctive way in which the light goes on and off.
2 Colour.
3 Period: the time taken for one complete cycle of the characteristic.
4 Elevation: the height of the light above Mean High Water Springs.
5 Range: the distance the light will 'throw' in normal visibility.

The last two, elevation and range, are not given for buoys (with the exception of Lanbys, which are considered as lightvessels). The strictest attention to the description of a light is necessary for its correct identification. A light must never be assumed to be the one looked for until its description has been tallied with the information on the chart. The description is printed alongside the light symbol on the chart in an abbreviated form. It is important to be able to decipher the abbreviations used.

Characteristic and Period

The salient features by which a light is identified are its characteristic and period. There are enough variations available to ensure that there is little chance of confusion, provided that the period is meticulously measured, ideally with a stop-watch.

The characteristics in common use are illustrated in the table on page 64. The table also shows the abbreviations used on charts and in light lists to describe characteristics. The international abbreviations were introduced in British charts and publications in 1980 and will progressively replace the older forms as new editions of charts are published.

There are two common errors to be avoided when dealing with light characteristics. The abbreviation F denotes a fixed light (it is unfortunate

Light Characters

This block is a reproduction of part of section K in 5011 "Symbols and Abbreviations used on Admiralty Charts." It shows the new international abbreviations which will begin to appear on Admiralty charts in 1980.

For an explanation of lights on IALA System "A" see L70 in chart 5011 or chart 5044.

Fathoms and Metric Charts

Ref. Nos.	CLASS OF LIGHT		International abbreviations	Older form (where different)	Illustration Period shown ————
21	**Fixed** *(steady light)*		F		
22	**Occulting** *(total duration of light more than dark)*				
22	*Single-occulting*		Oc	Occ	
27	*Group-occulting*	e.g.	Oc(2)	GpOcc(2)	
(Ka)	*Composite group-occulting*	e.g.	Oc(2+3)	GpOcc(2+3)	
23a	**Isophase** *(light and dark equal)*		Iso		
23	**Flashing** *(total duration of light less than dark)*				
23	*Single-flashing*		Fl		
(Kb)	*Long-flashing (flash 2s or longer)*		LFl		
28	*Group-flashing*	e.g.	Fl(3)	GpFl(3)	
(Kc)	*Composite group-flashing*	e.g.	Fl(2+1)	GpFl(2+1)	
24	**Quick** *(50 to 79—usually either 50 or 60—flashes per minute)*				
24	*Continuous quick*		Q	QkFl	
(Kd)	*Group quick*	e.g.	Q(3)	QkFl(3)	
25	*Interrupted quick*		IQ	IntQkFl	
(Ke)	**Very Quick** *(80 to 159—usually either 100 or 120—flashes per minute)*				
(Ke)	*Continuous very quick*		VQ	VQkFl	
(Kf)	*Group very quick*	e.g.	VQ(3)	VQkFl(3)	
(Kg)	*Interrupted very quick*		IVQ	IntVQkFl	
(Kh)	**Ultra Quick** *(160 or more—usually 240 to 300—flashes per minute)*				
(Kh)	*Continuous ultra quick*		UQ		
(Ki)	*Interrupted ultra quick*		IUQ		
30a	**Morse Code**	e.g.	Mo(K)		
29	**Fixed and Flashing**		FFl		
26	**Alternating**	e.g.	Al.WR	Alt.WR	

	COLOUR	International abbreviations	Older form (where different)	RANGE in sea miles	International abbreviations	Older form
67	White	W *(may be omitted)*		*Single range* e.g.	15M	
66	Red	R				
64	Green	G		*2 ranges* e.g.	14/12M	14,12M
(Kj)	Yellow	Y				
65	Orange	Y	Or	*3 or more ranges* e.g.	22-18M	22,20,18M
63	Blue	Bu	Bl			
61	Violet	Vi				
	ELEVATION is given in metres (m) or feet (ft)			**PERIOD** in seconds e.g.	5s	5sec

that F is also the initial letter of flashing and this sometimes causes confusion). The periods of lights with complex characteristics are also easily confused. For instance, the period of an alternating light covers the full cycle of both colours, not just the duration of one colour.

Multi-coloured Lights

Some lights exhibit more than one colour. In these cases, if white is one of the colours involved, it is mentioned in the description. There are two ways in which a light may exhibit more than one colour — alternating lights and sectored lights — and it is important to distinguish between them.

Alternating Lights: Different colours are shown in succession. In the description on the chart the characteristic is preceded by the abbreviation Al and is followed by the colours shown. Remember that such lights have the abbreviation Al before the characteristic and all the colours will be seen in the same sequence whenever the light is visible.

Sectored Lights: When a multi-coloured light is not alternating (when the abbreviation Al is not in the characteristic) it will be a sectored light.

Sectored lights show different colours in different geographical sectors. An observer will see only one colour of light while he is within a given sector, but if he sails into another sector the light will show a different colour (Fig 3.1, overleaf).

Sectors are used frequently to draw attention to dangers across which a light is visible. For instance, St Catherine's Point Lighthouse on the southern side of the Isle of Wight shows a white light over the greater part of the arc of visibility, but there is a red sector covering the dangers off the south-west coast of the island.

In the example in Fig 3.1 an observer will see:

In Sector A	Fl (2) W 15s
In Sector B	Fl (2) G 15s
In Sector C	Fl (2) R 15s

On large-scale charts suitable for coastal navigation the various sectors are shown by dotted lines and the colours indicated as shown in Fig 3.1. The chart should be examined carefully to find the different coloured sectors.

On small-scale charts the sectors may not be shown. In that case, the navigator must refer to a light list, where he will find the limits of the various sectors given as True Bearings from Seaward, that is, from the observer's point of view looking inward towards the light.

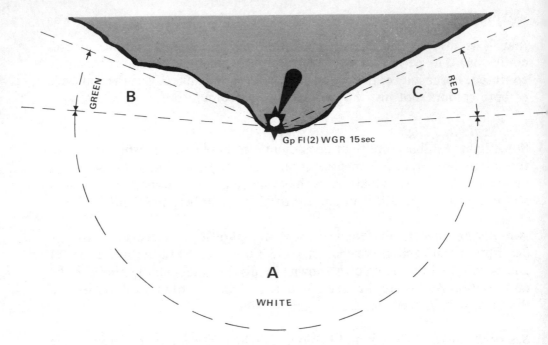

Fig 3.1 A sector light, as shown on a chart

Red 230°−280°, white 280°−070°, green 070°−100° means that the sectors are distributed as shown in Fig 3.2. Note carefully what is meant by 'bearings from seaward'.

Sometimes the terrain surrounding a light is such that over a certain sector the light is obscured (obscd). The obscured sectors are shown on the chart in the same way as coloured sectors.

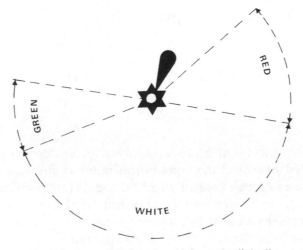

Fig 3.2 A sector light, plotted from the light list

Elevation and Range

The elevation of a light is the height of the focal plane of the light above the level of Mean High Water Springs. This height is given in metres (m) on a metric chart and feet (ft) on a fathom chart.

The elevation is important to navigation because it is one of the factors which determines the distance at which an observer will see the light. For a yachtsman navigating in normal visibility, it will probably be the main factor and its importance is thereby enhanced.

The geographical range of a light is the distance at which it can be seen, theoretically, neglecting the condition of visibility and the power of the light. It depends upon the height of the light and the observer's height of eye.

How far an observer sees a light over the curve of the horizon depends upon his own height of eye, which determines how far away his horizon is (the distance 'd' in Fig 3.3), and the height of the light determines the distance d_1 or d_2 in the figure. The higher the light the greater this distance. (Chapter 5 deals with using geographical range for fixing position.)

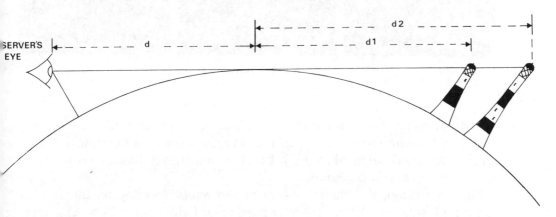

Fig 3.3 Geographical range

The range of a light given in its description on the chart is not the geographical range but the nominal range, and takes into account only the power of the light and the condition of the atmosphere. In perfect conditions of visibility the power of the light will determine how far it will 'throw'. When visibility is reduced, the 'throw' will be less. This distance, which depends on the power of the light and the prevailing condition of the atmosphere, is called the luminous range.

The nominal range, which is charted, is the luminous range when the state of the atmosphere is such that normal visibility is 10 sea miles. It is the distance at which an observer can expect to see the light in normal conditions of good visibility, if his height of eye is great enough.

Loom

In certain conditions of the atmosphere a light will be seen while it is still well below the horizon by virtue of its loom. Loom is defined as the diffused glow observed from a light below the horizon owing to atmospheric scattering. It is a common phenomenon and very useful. If the loom is seen while the light is still well below the horizon, it appears something like a searchlight, sweeping across the sky near the horizon. As the light comes nearer to the horizon, the arc of sweep becomes smaller until finally the light itself breaks the horizon. It is then at 'dipping distance' (Fig 3.4).

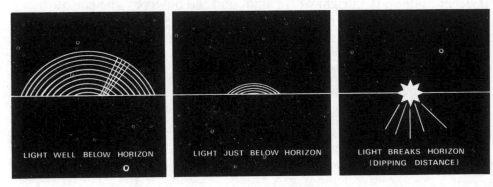

LIGHT WELL BELOW HORIZON

LIGHT JUST BELOW HORIZON

LIGHT BREAKS HORIZON (DIPPING DISTANCE)

Fig 3.4 The loom of a light

A preliminary check on the identity of the light can be made by counting the flashes as the loom from each one sweeps across the horizon, but this cannot be relied upon absolutely because sometimes flashes miss and a wrong characteristic is counted.

Care in reading the chart is necessary to avoid forming an incomplete picture of what is shown from a particular light source. For example, Dungeness Lighthouse is charted as Fl 10s 40m 27M, FRG 37m 11M. Careful reading indicates that there are, in fact, two lights shown from the lighthouse. One flashing white every 10 seconds, 40m high with a range of 27 miles, and another which is a fixed light showing red and green sectors, 37m high, with a range of 11 miles (Fig 3.5).

An observer in either of the two red sectors would see the flashing white light and, below it, a fixed red light. In the green sector he would see the flashing white light and a fixed green light below it. Anywhere else, he would see only the white flashing light.

Sometimes with a multi-coloured light, one colour will be visible further than the others in which case two ranges will be given. For example, Fl WR 10s 35m, 17, 15M. The first range given, in this case 17 miles, belongs to the first colour, white, and the second, 15 miles, to the red.

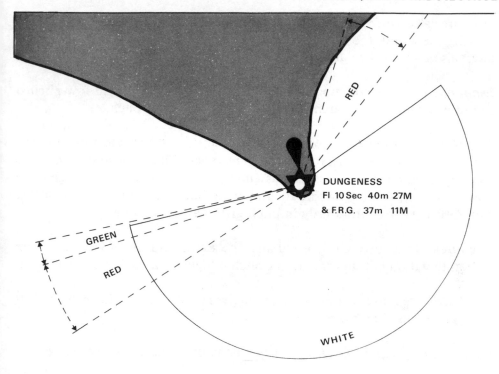

Fig 3.5 Dungeness light

Other Lights and Abbreviations

Aero Lights These are mainly for the use of aircraft but are very often visible at sea. They are usually very powerful lights and may be seen at great distances, particularly when the loom is visible. The characteristic is often given on the chart, for example, Aero Alt RG. It must be remembered that these lights are primarily for use of aircraft and if the characteristic is changed it may be some time before mariners are notified.

Fog-detector Lights (Fog-detr Lt) A few lighthouses are fitted with these lights, which are additional to the navigational light, for automatic detection of fog. They emit a bluish-coloured flash, of powerful intensity and sweep continuously along the horizon and back.

Fog Signals

Fog signals are sounded from the same sources as the lights just described — that is, from lighthouses, lightvessels and buoys. They, too, have character-istics which are printed on the chart, usually below the light characteristic from the same source. As in the case of lights, it is important to identify the characteristic of a given fog signal if it is to be of any value. The description,

69

in abbreviated form, gives the type of apparatus and may be used to help identify the sound, the number of blasts emitted as a group, and the regular intervals at which they are sounded.

Diaphone (Dia) uses compressed air. It gives a very powerful low-pitched sound and ends with an unmistakable 'grunt' of lower pitch.

Fog Horn (Horn) uses compressed air or electricity to vibrate a diaphragm. The sound produced varies with different types. The most important ones combine a number of simultaneous emitters, at different pitches, giving a powerful blast, something like the diaphone but without the 'grunt' at the end. Others vary continuously in pitch giving a 'wavy' note.

Fog Siren (Siren) uses compressed air. The sound and the power vary from station to station but, in general, the pitch is higher than a diaphone or horn.

Fog Reed (Reed) uses compressed air. It gives a weak, high-pitched sound. It is very often used at harbour entrances.

Explosive Fog Signal (Explos) makes a bang by firing explosive charges.

Fog Bell (Bell), Fog Gong (Gong), Fog Whistle (Whis) These signals are given from buoys. They may be operated mechanically or by wave action. The sound emitted is indicated by the name. If operation is mechanical, the sound will be regular but if by wave action, it will be irregular. For example, Bell (2) 10s indicates 2 strokes on a bell every 10 seconds. The precise nature of this information means that the bell must be mechanically operated. When no such detailed information is given, for example, Bell, it is to be assumed that the operation is by wave action and the sounding of the bell will be irregular. The same applies to gongs and whistles.

Some buoys have what is called a reserve fog signal. The characteristic might be stated as Horn (2) 60s Whis. This indicates that in addition to a horn sounding 2 blasts every 60 seconds the buoy has a wave actuated whistle.

Examples of fog signals:

Dia (3) 60s	3 blasts on a diaphone every minute.
Horn 30s	1 blast on a fog horn every 30 seconds.
Dia Mo (A) 60s	Diaphone sounding morse letter 'A' every minute.
Siren (1 + 2) 60s	Siren sounding 1 blast followed at a short interval by 2 blasts and this composite group repeated every minute.

70

Sound in Fog

Sound in fog may travel erratically causing some confusion and anxiety if the limitations in picking up fog signals are not understood. The direction from which a fog signal comes is particularly affected and no precise bearing of the sound should be relied upon. Usually it is possible to determine that a fog signal is roughly ahead, on the bow, before the beam, roughly abeam, just abaft the beam, etc. Sometimes the direction can be defined a little more closely, but an attempt at precision would not be realistic.

The distance at which a fog signal may be heard is also erratic. It is possible in certain conditions to pick up a powerful diaphone on a lightvessel at 8 miles, only to lose it at 7 miles, pick it up again at 3 miles, lose it 5 minutes later and not hear it again although passing quite close. Hearing the sound at a distance greater than expected can cause as much anxiety as silence when it is thought to be well within range. It is possible to approach a lightvessel in fog and pass within ½ mile of it without hearing a sound, only to be deafened by the roar of its diaphone close astern as it is passed.

Despite these limitations, fog signals are very helpful and as much care and attention should be given to picking them up and identifying them as is given to picking up and identifying lights in clear weather.

If under power when trying to pick up a fog signal it is advisable to stop the engine at intervals. The sound of the signal will be heard much sooner and more definitely in a surrounding silence. This applies also during an offshore passage among shipping traffic. The fog signals of any vessels in the vicinity are more easily heard if the engine is quiet at times. Fog signals from shipping are unlikely to be mistaken for the navigational fog signals just described. They have a different quality, are lighter, steadier and shorter, and their directions are likely to change relatively quickly. However, the possibility of confusion adds to the importance of knowing and recognising the characteristic of whichever navigational fog signal is being sought.

Inshore and Estuary Marks

Buoys and beacons are used in estuaries and inshore waters to mark the limits of navigable channels, shoals, wrecks, dangers and other features.

IALA Buoyage

Every buoy carries identity symbols which denote its particular function. These are its shape, colour, top-mark and light characteristic. The system of coding is a standard one throughout European waters. It is known as the IALA system and was introduced in 1977 by the International Association of Lighthouse Authorities.

There are three families of marker: lateral, used to indicate the sides of a defined navigable channel; cardinal, which mark the edges of shoals or other hazards and junctions or bends in channels in relation to the cardinal points of the compass; and four other marks which are neither lateral nor cardinal in nature.

Lateral buoys are named port hand and starboard hand in accordance with the sides on which they should be left. Using sides in the way it is necessary to establish the direction of buoyage and by convention, this is *into* harbour where there is an obvious harbour approach channel and around continental land masses in a clockwise direction. Thus, the direction of buoyage is around the British Isles from the SW to NE. Where there is any possibility of doubt the direction is marked on the chart.

Cardinal buoys are named in accordance with the side of the feature on which they are placed. For example, a north cardinal buoy marks the north side of a shoal.

The shapes, colours, top-marks and light characteristics of the various buoys are shown on the following four pages. They should be memorised so that as soon as a buoy is sighted its message is immediately clear.

Buoys are not intended to be a complete system of navigation, replacing charts; they are an aid to navigation, supplementing the charts. The only exceptions to this rule are small harbours, where the sea bed is unstable and the position of the approach channel changes. If the deep water is marked by buoys which are moved to conform to the shape of the channel, the only way to enter harbour is to rely on the buoys.

There are a number of features of IALA buoyage which are designed to make the characteristics easy to remember. With the lateral buoys the red to port, green to starboard convention is logical.

All cardinal buoys have a double-cone top-mark. Points up indicating North and points down for South are logical. The West mark with points together looks like a W on its side, which leaves only points apart for East. The black and yellow colouring conforms to the top-marks, if one remembers that the points of the cones show where the black is.

The isolated danger mark is almost one of the cardinal marks, in that it has a double top-mark and horizontal stripes, with red for danger.

The light characteristics of cardinal buoys conform to a clock code: 3 flashes at 3 o'clock (East), 6 at 6 o'clock (South), and so on.

Minor Channels

Minor channels in creeks and small harbours of little commercial importance are often marked with withies and perches. These may conform to the lateral marking convention, red to port and green to starboard, but they may be just poles or tree branches. They are likely to mark the deep channel, but the term deep in this context is a relative one; it may be a matter of less drying height in the channel than out of it. The fact that a channel is marked does not mean that there is enough water to sail in it. Even if there is enough water in the centre of the channel it is highly likely that the marks will be on the

THE IALA MARITIME BUOYAGE SYSTEM

LATERAL MARKS

Lateral marks are used to mark the sides of navigable channels, red cans to port, green cones to starboard.

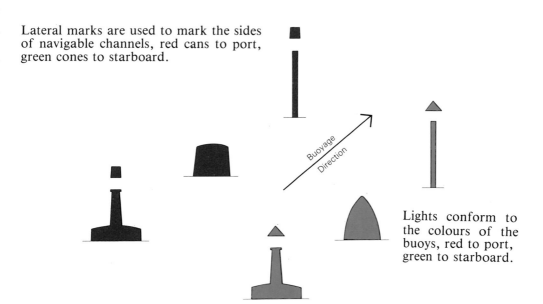

Lights conform to the colours of the buoys, red to port, green to starboard.

The salient distinguishing feature of a lateral buoy is its colour. The shape, of either the buoy or its topmark, is also distinctive.

MODIFIED LATERAL MARKS

Preferred channel to the right

Light, composite group flashing red (eg Fl (2 + 1) R)

Preferred channel to the left

Light, composite group flashing green (eg Fl (2 + 1) G)

Modified lateral marks were introduced early in 1981. Their purpose is to mark the point where a channel divides, when proceeding in the conventional direction of buoyage, and indicate the preferred channel. They are unlikely to be widely used in U.K. waters

CARDINAL MARKS

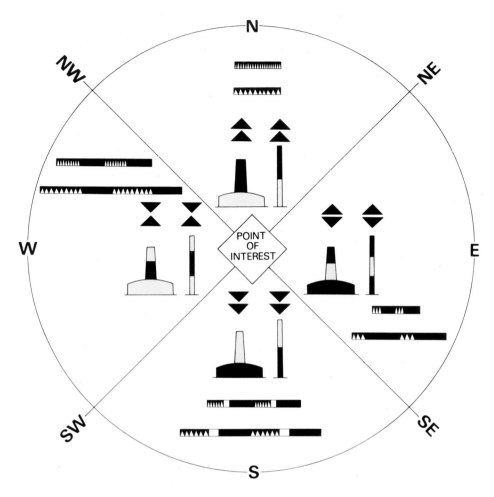

Cardinal marks are named according to the side of the hazard, or point of interest, which they mark. The west side of a shoal will be marked with a west cardinal buoy. This convention is the opposite to the naming of lateral buoys which are named according to the side of the navigable channel on which they are placed.

The salient distinguishing feature of any cardinal mark is its double-cone topmark. The arrangement of topmarks is easily remembered: North, points up; South, points down; West, points together (*W*est, *W*oman's *W*aist); East, points apart (*E*ast, *E*quitorially *E*nlarged).

The arrangement of the yellow and black horizontal bands has a logic which follows that of the topmarks — the points of the cone topmark indicate where the black will be on the body of the buoy.

The light characteristics conform to a clock code: East (3 o'clock) 3 flashes; South (6 o'clock) 6 flashes; West (9 o'clock) 9 flashes; North (12 flashes would be uncountable) continuous flashing (South is actually six flashes plus a long flash to make it easier to distinguish from east and west).

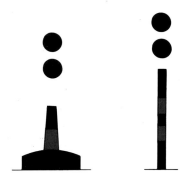

ISOLATED DANGER MARKS

Used to mark an isolated danger, with navigable water all round.

The salient distinguishing feature is the double-sphere topmark. The double topmark is a feature which it shares with the marks of the cardinal family — it might be considered as a centre cardinal mark.

The light characteristic is group flashing 2

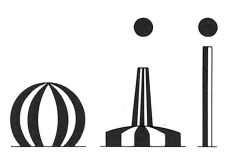

SAFE WATER MARKS

Safe water marks are used as landfall buoys or as centre-channel markers — there is deep water all around them.

The single topmark is a feature which it shares with marks of the lateral family — it might be considered as a centre lateral mark.

The light characteristic is white, isophase or occulting or one long flash every 10s or Morse 'A'

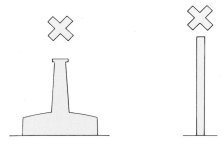

SPECIAL MARKS

Special marks are not primarily intended to assist navigation but indicate special areas or features such as military exercise areas, recreation areas and spoil grounds. They may be any shape, are always yellow and may carry a yellow X topmark.

If they carry a light it will be yellow and of a characteristic which does not conflict with the characteristic of a navigational mark

BUOYAGE OF AN ESTUARY

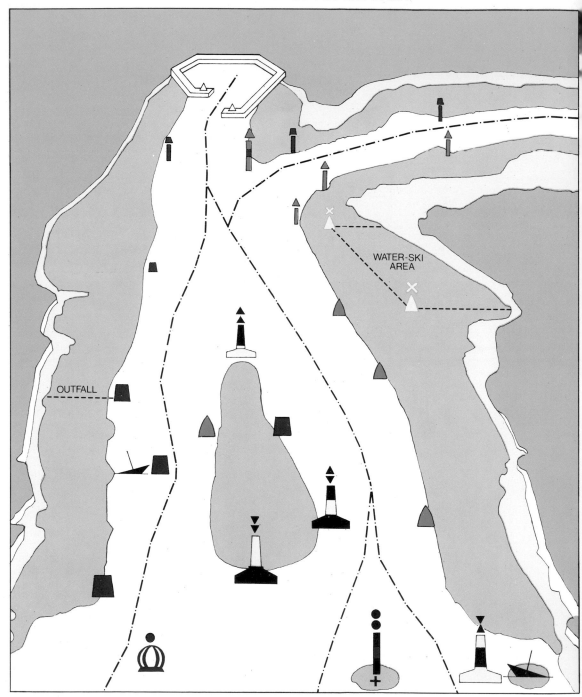

Note that lateral, cardinal and other marks are integrated in the system. There is no convention which requires that lateral marks alone must be used in a channel, cardinal marks may be introduced to draw attention to features such as junctions or bends.

shallow side of the low-water mark; it is much easier to dig them in just above low water than just below.

Offshore Marks

Visual aids to offshore navigation consist of lighthouses, lightvessels, Lanbys and ordinary buoys.

Lighthouses are familiar to everyone. They are erected on prominent headlands and in some cases on off-lying rocks and islets. They carry powerful lights at a considerable height above sea-level and are invaluable long-range aids to navigation.

Lightvessels are positioned to mark shoal waters extending well offshore where lighthouses cannot be used. The navigational light is 12m (40ft) above sea-level (Fig 3.6).

British lightvessels are red in colour and have their names painted in white along their sides. Foreign lightvessels have the same general appearance with their names painted on the side, but are not necessarily red. Lightvessels carry a white anchor light on the forestay like an ordinary vessel at anchor in addition to the navigational light. Lightvessels are withdrawn for servicing from time to time when they are replaced either by a relief lightvessel or by an

Fig 3.6 A typical lightvessel

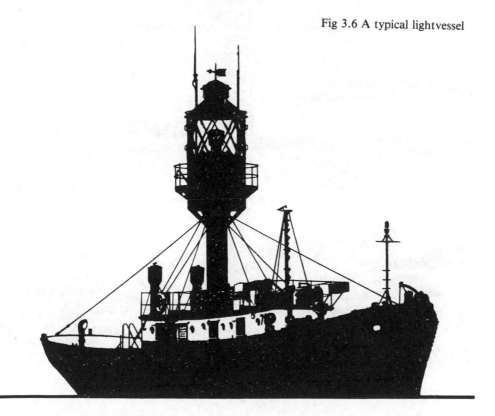

73

ordinary buoy. Details of any such change are promulgated in *Notices to Mariners* and, for regular seasonal changes, in the light list. Full descriptions of all lightvessels are given in the *Admiralty List of Lights*.

A Lanby (Large Automatic Navigational Buoy) is used in a similar way to a lightvessel. It was the intention that Lanbys would replace all lightvessels, but difficulty in maintaining them (the base is hemispherical in shape and the motion in a sea-way is too much for even the strongest stomach), has led to delays in the planned change-over.

These buoys consist of a discus-shaped base 12m (40ft) in diameter supporting a deck cone holding a trellis mast with the navigational light at

Fig 3.7 A typical Lanby

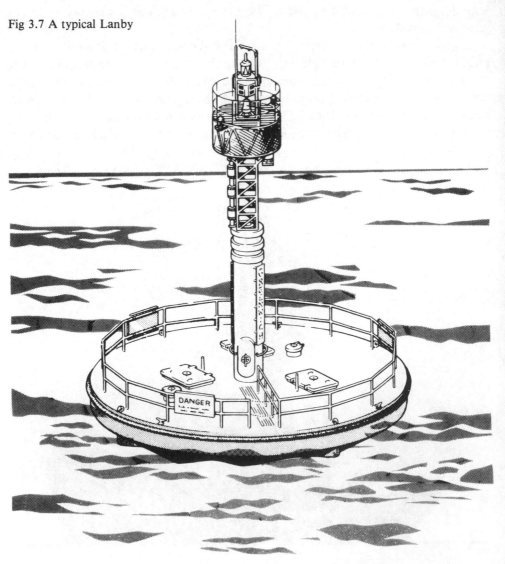

the top (Fig 3.7). The light is 12m (40ft) above sea-level, which is the same as the height of the light on a standard lightvessel. It is controlled by a daylight sensing switch. Lanbys are monitored by a shore control station which can take care of up to five such buoys.

Ordinary buoys are found offshore mainly in areas such as the Dover Straits and southern North Sea where there are numerous shoals which require the marking of deep-water channels. There is little difference between them and the buoys used inshore except that they tend to be larger, particularly in the case of their top-marks.

Navigation in Marked Channels

Inshore waters, estuaries, harbour approach channels and well-marked offshore deep-water channels pose special navigational problems for the yachtsman. In areas such as the Thames Estuary, where there are shoals extending many miles offshore and fast tidal streams, and the Dover Straits where there are heavy concentrations of shipping, the navigational priorities are rather different from those which apply around the rest of our coast.

Narrow Channels

The fact that a deep-water channel is well buoyed means that it is likely to be much used by large ships. Even if such a channel is a mile or so in width, to a large ship it will be regarded as a narrow channel to which Rule 9 of the *International Regulations for Preventing Collisions at Sea* applies. This rule states:

(a) A vessel proceeding along the course of a narrow channel or fairway shall keep as near to the outer limit of the channel or fairway which lies on her starboard side as is safe and practicable.

(b) A vessel of less than 20 metres in length or a sailing vessel shall not impede the passage of a vessel which can safely navigate only within a narrow channel or fairway.

(c) A vessel engaged in fishing shall not impede the passage of any other vessel navigating within a narrow channel or fairway.

(d) A vessel shall not cross a narrow channel or fairway if such crossing impedes the passage of a vessel which can safely navigate only within such channel or fairway. The latter vessel may use the sound signal prescribed in Rule 34 (d) if in doubt as to the intention of the crossing vessel.

(e) (i) In a narrow channel or fairway when overtaking can take place only if the vessel to be overtaken has to take action to permit safe passing, the vessel intending to overtake shall indicate her intention by sounding the appropriate signal prescribed in Rule 34 (c) (i). The vessel to be overtaken shall, if in agreement, sound the appropriate signal prescribed in Rule 34 (c) (ii) and take steps to permit safe passing. If in doubt she may sound the signals prescribed in Rule 34 (d).

(ii) This Rule does not relieve the overtaking vessel of her obligation under Rule 13.

(f) A vessel nearing a bend or an area of a narrow channel or fairway where other vessels may be obscured by an intervening obstruction shall navigate with particular alertness and caution and shall sound the appropriate signal prescribed in Rule 34 (e).

(g) Any vessel shall, if the circumstances of the case admit, avoid anchoring in a narrow channel.

Paragraph 9 (b) is important. The best way to comply with it is to keep outside the marked channel, which is often easy because there is likely to be a considerable distance between the edge of the buoyed channel and water shallow enough to be a hazard to a yacht. If it is necessary to sail along or across a channel it is vital to keep a particularly good look-out and move to the edge of the channel on the approach of a larger ship.

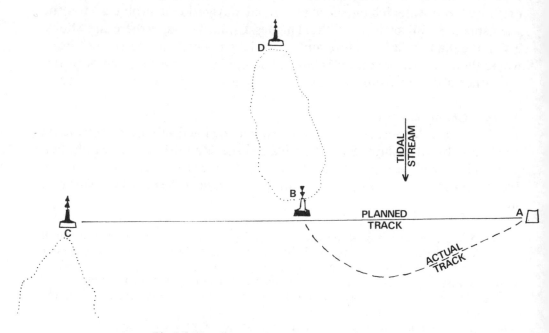

Fig 3.8 The danger of over-relying on buoys

Buoy Hopping

Buoy hopping is navigation made simple. It consists of planning a course from one buoy to the next so that there is always a navigational mark in sight ahead or astern. The danger is that it looks too simple.

The commonest error in buoy hopping is shown in Fig 3.8. A yacht sets out from the red can buoy at A on a passage which is to take her past the south side of a shoal, B, and on round the north side of another shoal, C. Shortly after leaving A, she picks up the south cardinal buoy at B and steers for it. Between A and B she is being set south by a strongish tidal stream so she actually arrives at B heading north instead of west. Fine on the starboard bow is a north cardinal buoy, D, assumed to be the next mark, so she sets out towards it, with disastrous results. No one thought to look on the port beam for the buoy at C which is really the next mark.

There are three easy ways to avoid this trap. First, check the tidal-stream atlas to see which way and how strongly the stream is setting. Second, note the compass course to make sure that it tallies with the charted direction of the next buoy and that the yacht is not wandering off course. Finally, do not navigate relative to a single mark. Check that all the buoys which should be visible are in their expected places. In this particular example, final disaster might have been avoided by periodic checks on the depth by echo-sounder. The rapid shoaling after passing buoy B might have shown that all was not well before the yacht grounded.

Just as it is a mistake to rely only on buoys, it is a mistake to ignore visual aids to navigation. The direct line between port of departure and destination may lead just out of sight of a number of buoys or lightships. By making a slight detour from the direct line it would be possible to keep track of position throughout the passage and this is likely to be a good idea. If the visibility closes in on a yacht which has been without a positive check or position for several hours, she is in a much more difficult position than if she had been able to check her position 30 minutes earlier.

4 Position Lines and Fixing

The Need for Position Fixing

The open sea is, for all practical purposes, featureless. There can be no question of orientation at sea in the sense in which it is possible to orientate oneself ashore by reference to landmarks in the immediate vicinity, because there is usually nothing visible in the immediate vicinity except water. Position finding at sea has to be carried out by reference to relatively distant features, so a special technique known as position fixing is required.

A position fix is derived from a number of position lines. A position line is a line on which the yacht is known to be. A position fix is the point of intersection of two or more position lines. It is sound practice whenever possible to include three position lines in a fix so that it is to some extent self-checking, any gross error being revealed by the fact that the three lines do not intersect at anything like a point.

There are two possible reasons for fixing position. First, it may have been some time since the yacht's position was last established with any degree of accuracy and a fix is needed simply to find out where she is. In this case the aim is to establish position, but there is always the possibility of an error, which may not be immediately apparent. It is sound practice to make a habit of noting the depth by echo-sounder at the same time as the fix is taken as a check against gross errors in the fix. The second reason for a fix is to establish or confirm the course and speed being made good. For this purpose a minimum of two fixes, with a substantial interval between them, is required.

It is important to remember that a fix does not establish the yacht's present position; it established a position at a time now past when the bearings were observed. It is a waste of time to take a fix unless a future position is projected ahead, either as a DR or EP, to confirm that the present course and speed are safe.

Sources of Position Lines and Fixes

There are a number of sources of position lines, of varying degrees of accuracy.

78

POSITION LINE BY COMPASS BEARING

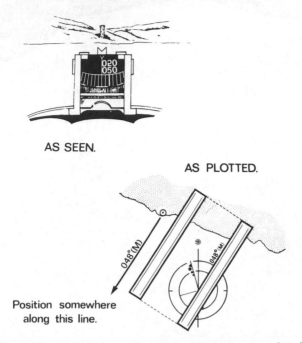

AS SEEN.

AS PLOTTED.

Position somewhere
along this line.

Fig 4.1 Establishing a visual position line by compass bearing

Visual Position Lines

A visual position line is derived from a magnetic (or compass) bearing of a conspicuous charted object (Fig 4.1). It is the position line most commonly used for fixing during coastal navigation.

On any stretch of coast there are usually likely to be three objects visible which can be used to provide three visual position lines for a fix. Sometimes there are many more than three objects visible, in which case it is necessary to select the most suitable. Each object used should be unambiguously identifiable, both visually and on the chart. The angle of cut between each pair of position lines should be no less than 30° and no more than 150°; if a finer angle of cut is used, any error in either bearing results in a relatively large displacement of the fix position (Fig 4.2, overleaf). Objects should be chosen so that their distance from the yacht is as short as possible; the greater the distance the larger is the displacement of the position line resulting from any error in the bearing. Care should be taken in using edges of land; a gently shelving edge may not appear as an edge at all at low water and at any distance the true edge may be below the visible horizon. Buoys should be used with caution, particularly off exposed coasts as there is always a possibility of a buoy dragging out of position.

When taking visual bearings with a hand-bearing compass, it is important to check that the compass is not held close to any ferrous metal or electrical

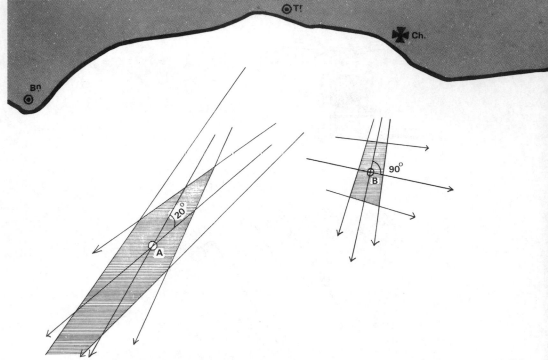

Fig 4.2 The effect of a small error in observation on a fix with a narrow angle between position lines (A) and a 90° angle of cut (B)

POSITION LINE BY TRANSIT

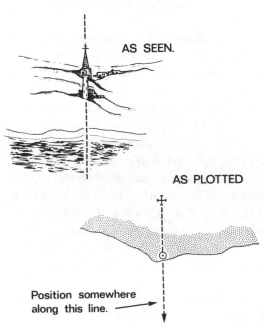

AS SEEN.

AS PLOTTED

Position somewhere along this line.

Fig 4.3 Establishing a position line from a transit

equipment which will have a deviating effect. Metal guard-rail stanchions, galvanised standing rigging and instrument display panels are all likely to be positioned close to convenient places in which to use the hand-bearing compass. It is also possible for steel-framed spectacles to have marked deviating effect.

Transits

A transit is the alignment of two conspicuous charted objects (Fig 4.3). It is, therefore, a special type of visual position line, with the advantage that it does not depend upon the accuracy of a hand-bearing compass. The greater the horizontal distance between the objects the more accurate is the position line which they give. If the two objects are very close together, it is extremely difficult to judge whether or not they are exactly in line. Two sets of transits will seldom line up simultaneously, so while a transit may be included in a fix it is unlikely that a fix will be obtained from two simultaneous transits.

Radio Bearings

The use of radio direction-finders has already been explained in Chapter 2. Radio bearings can be plotted to obtain a fix in exactly the same way as visual bearings, but as the distances involved are generally much greater proportionally less accuracy is obtainable.

Depth-contour Lines

A depth-contour line can be used to obtain a position line, using a lead line or echo-sounder. The accuracy of such a position line depends very much upon the definition of the contours of the sea bed. If the bottom is gently shelving the contour lines will be ill-defined and inaccurate as position lines. With a steeply shelving sea bed, contour lines can be an extremely accurate source of positional information.

The 'Line of Soundings' Fix

A depth-contour line can produce only a single position line but a series of soundings can give, under certain circumstances, an absolute fix. The method involves taking soundings over a period of time and noting the time and log reading at each significant change of depth. The soundings can then be plotted along a straight edge of paper, at the scale of the chart in use, making the appropriate allowance for tidal set. The paper edge is then aligned to the course made good and positioned on the chart so that the soundings, reduced to chart datum, match the charted depths (Fig 4.4, overleaf). The method works only where the sea bed has a distinctive shape, and there is often a danger of ambiguity. However, it can be a useful source of information, particularly when poor visibility imposes restrictions on the

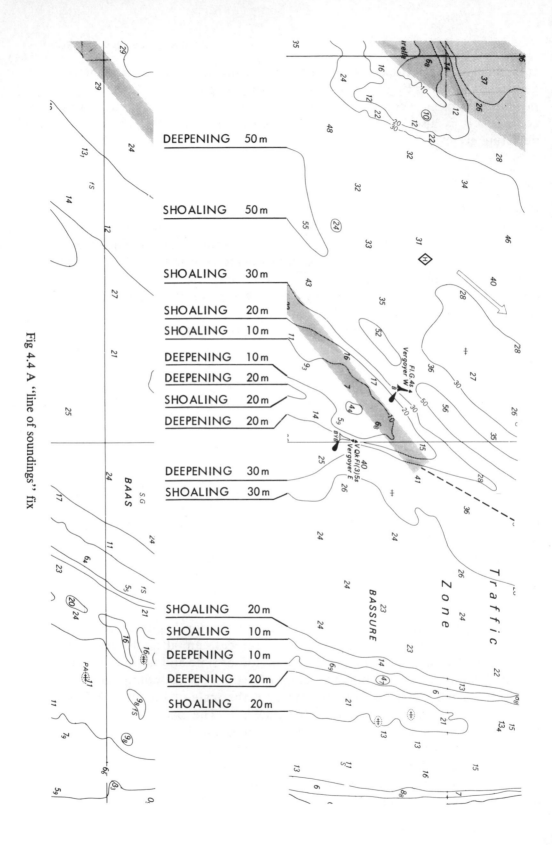

Fig 4.4 A "line of soundings" fix

availability of other fixing methods. There are very few places where the shape of the sea bed allows an absolute fix to be obtained by a series of soundings, but it is often possible to establish an area in which the yacht must be, thereby confirming an EP as free from major errors.

Horizontal Angle Fixes

The horizontal angle fix depends on the fact that the angles subtended at the circumference of a circle by any cord are equal. Thus, an observation of the angle between two objects gives rise to a position circle. A position circle is a perfectly good form of position line, the fact that it is curved instead of straight being no disadvantage. If the two angles between three marks are observed, two position circles result and a fix is given by their intersection (Fig 4.5). It is reasonably easy to find the centre of each circle of position. (The angle at the centre of the circle subtended by the cord on which the two objects lie is twice the angle subtended at the circumference. The angles at the base of the isosceles triangle formed by the cord and the two radii from the centre to the extremities of the cord are each [180 − angle at the centre] ÷ 2.) In practice, it is much simpler not to draw the position circles but to plot the two observed angles on a Douglas protractor or tracing paper and lay the trace over the chart so that each line passes through the corresponding observed mark. The position is then at the point from which the angles are plotted. A special plotting instrument called a station pointer

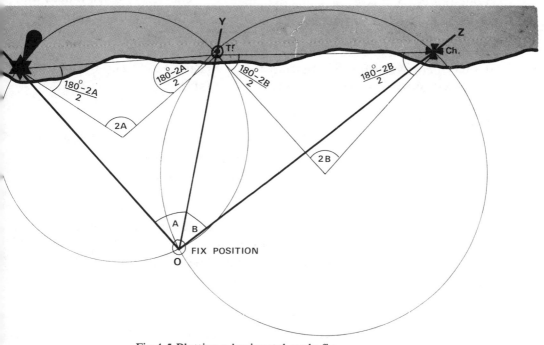

Fig 4.5 Plotting a horizontal angle fix

simplifies the plotting still further. The station pointer has one fixed arm and two movable arms which can be set to the required angles. The instrument is then laid on the chart with the arms passing through the observed marks and the position plotted at the centre of the instrument.

It is possible to obtain an extremely accurate fix by measuring horizontal angles with a sextant,* to a tolerance of 1 minute of arc compared with the 1° or 2° tolerance of a compass.

A horizontal angle fix can also be taken with a bearing sight on a steering compass. This is a useful way to check the deviation of the steering compass, comparing the plotted position as a horizontal angle fix and as a three-bearing visual fix. The former is independent of deviation, provided that the heading remained the same while the bearings were taken and it should be possible to adjust the three visual bearings by applying the same correction to each magnetic bearing to give two coincident positions. The correction applied is the deviation on that heading.

Although three fixing marks are used in a horizontal angle fix, only two position lines result. It is therefore not a self-checking fix and any observational or plotting error will simply displace the plotted position.

Position Lines from Range Circles

Any measurement of distance from a charted mark will give a circle of position. Range can be measured by vertical sextant angle,* radar or optical range-finder. A special case of range measurement occurs when a light dips below or rises above the horizon, enabling its range to be found from a table of rising and dipping distances, such as that contained in yachtsmen's nautical almanacs. Both the height of eye of the observer and the height of the light, corrected for difference between charted height and height of tide below MHWS, must be known to enter the table.

Mixed Fixes

There is no reason why position lines from different sources should not be used to give a fix. For instance, two bearings observed at the time of crossing a depth-contour line can give a good three position line fix.

Pre-plotted Fixes

It is possible to pre-plot fixes by drawing a bearing lattice. In large ships this technique is sometimes used in narrow channels where rapid fixing is needed for exact positioning in the deepest water. The advantage is that observed bearings can be plotted rapidly and, with practice, it is possible to plot the

*A knowledge of the use of a sextant is not required of candidates for the Yachtmaster Offshore Certificate. If a sextant is to be used for terrestrial navigation, it must be tested for index error, side error and perpendicularity, and any errors found must be removed.

position on the chart within seconds of taking the last bearing. In theory, the technique should be useful to the short-handed skipper who wants to be able to plot a position without spending any length of time at the chart table. In practice, however, pre-drawing the bearing lattice is time-consuming and a certain amount of practice is required in using the lattice before there is any significant reduction in plotting times. The technique is useful, however, for plotting radio fixes, where it may be difficult to spread the chart out to plot the bearings. A lattice for radio bearings is shown in Fig 4.6.

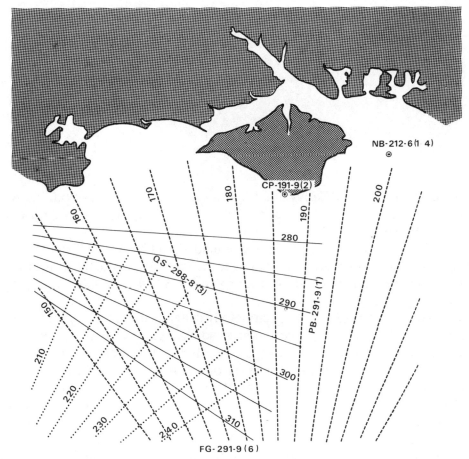

Fig 4.6 A bearing lattice for radio fixing

Transferred Position Line Fixes
If only one identifiable object is visible, it may be possible to use it to give an adequate fix. The method, known as a running fix is best explained by an example, shown overleaf in Fig 4.7.

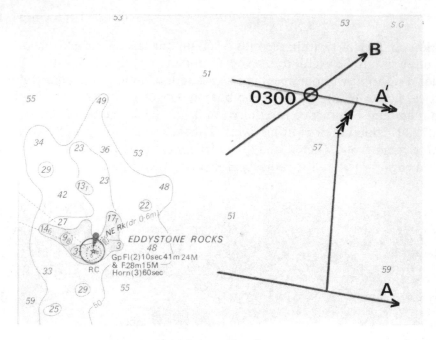

Fig 4.7 A running fix

At 0200 a bearing of Eddystone Lighthouse is observed (position line A). An hour later, at 0300, a second bearing of Eddystone Lighthouse is observed (position line B).

Provided that the course and distance made good between 0200 and 0300 are known, the first position line can be transferred (A¹ in the illustration) by the appropriate direction and distance to give a fix where it cuts the second position line.

This type of fix is of limited accuracy. It depends upon the accuracy with which the course and distance made good between the two bearings are known. The argument on which it is based is that the yacht is on line A at 0200, so at 0300 she must be somewhere on the transferred position line A¹. There must, of course, be sufficient change of bearing between the two position lines to give a good angle of cut for the running fix. There is no reason why the method should not be applied to bearings of different marks with a time interval between them.

There are a number of special cases of transferred position line fix, such as 'doubling the angle on the bow', which can occasionally be used under special circumstances. In each of them it would be possible to plot a running fix exactly as described above, and the actual work involved is reduced very little by using the method which can be applied only to the special case. These methods are therefore of little more than academic interest to the yacht navigator who usually has more than just the navigation to cope with and seldom wishes to be tied to taking bearings at exact times and ensuring that

86

all the necessary conditions are fulfilled to be able to use the geometrically elegant special cases.

The one special type of transferred position line fix which has a practical use is the 'four point and abeam bearing' (Fig 4.8). When approaching a headland, the time and log reading are noted when the headland is 45° off the bow. Time and log reading are again noted when the headland is abeam, at which time the distance off will be the same as the distance run between the two bearings. This distance run is log reading corrected for tidal stream. The fix is valid only if there is no cross-component of tidal stream, but as this is often the case when rounding a headland the method does have its uses.

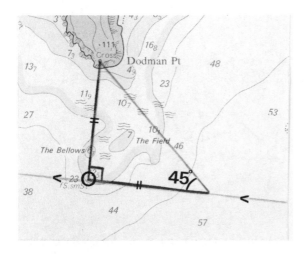

Fig 4.8 A four point and abeam bearing fix

Errors in Fixes

A three position line fix seldom plots as three lines intersecting at a point. The methods by which position lines are obtained do not have the inherent accuracy for that to occur, other than by chance. The triangle which is usually formed by three position lines is known as a cocked hat and, provided that it is not too large, it does not show an error in the fix. It is simply the natural result of using three position lines obtained with instruments which are not 100 per cent accurate.

The position of a fix should be taken as the point of intersection which will put the yacht closest to danger as she continues along her track. If a very large cocked hat occurs, showing that there is a definite mistake in one of the position lines, the fix should be retaken and plotted. Mistakes which commonly occur are the misidentification of one of the marks, misreading the compass, usually by 10°, misplotting a bearing by 10°, using the hand-bearing compass in a position where it is affected by ferrous metal or electrical equipment, or simply by applying variation the wrong way. At times there is a temptation to 'bend' the position lines so that the fix looks

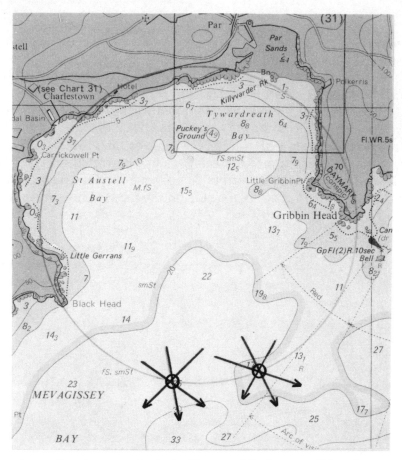

Fig 4.9 A circular fix. Either position looks like a good fix, but one of them has been obtained by applying the variation wrongly

better than it really is, to assume that a similar mark has been observed because it fits better than the one which it was originally thought to be, or to ignore one position line because it does not fit the navigator's general impression of where he thinks he is. There is no point in that sort of navigational 'cookery' — it proves nothing and can be extremely dangerous.

One special case sometimes occurs which destroys the self-checking nature of the three bearing visual fix. This is the so-called circular fix, in which all three marks and the yacht are on the circumference of a circle (Fig 4.9). The geometry of this situation is such that any error applied to all three bearings still gives rise to an apparently perfect fix. For instance, in the illustration the wrong application of a variation of 8°W moves the fix position a considerable distance, but the plot still looks correct.

The necessary conditions for a circular fix rarely occur and they can be avoided by ensuring that the centre of the three marks selected is closer to the yacht than the other two.

The Use of Single-position Lines
Leading Lines
The most common use of a single position line is as a leading line, into or out of a harbour. The line may be derived from a transit or bearing. It indicates the safe water through which the harbour entrance can be approached and the navigator knows that as long as he remains on the line he is safe; he is less concerned with his distance along the line.

A transit is very much easier to use as a leading line than a single mark giving a compass bearing. In a number of instances, leading lines are shown on the chart and, where the line is on a single object, it is nearly always possible to find a second object, even if it is only a street lamp or a tree which stands out as a distinctive shape or colour, to use as the second mark for a transit. It is sound practice to make a habit of converting single mark leading lines into transits by the use of uncharted but unambiguously identifiable second marks. Once a transit has been established, it is much easier to see if the yacht is drifting off the leading line and make the necessary course correction to bring her back on to the planned track.

When using a compass bearing as a leading line it is possible to become confused as to the correct way to turn to regain the line when off track. For instance, if the correct bearing of a mark ahead should be 252°(M) but the mark actually bears 250°(M), to which side of the line has the yacht drifted? The easiest way to decide is to look along the bearing of 252°(M). The compass will show that the line 252°(M) from the yacht passes to starboard of the head mark, so the yacht is obviously to starboard of the planned track. (A contributory factor to the confusion may be that the yacht is not actually steering 252°(M) but, say, 260°(M) to counteract the effect of tidal stream setting across the track.)

Using a mark astern can be even more confusing, but the same system can sort out the situation. If the stern mark should bear 252°(M) (the leading line away from it, and therefore the required track being 072°(M)), but the mark actually bears 250°(M), it is difficult to make an instant appraisal of the side of the line to which the yacht has been set. Again, looking along the required bearing of 252°(M) will show that this line passes to port of the stern mark. A little extra concentration is required in order to remember that the port side is the port side, whether one is looking ahead or astern. In terms of right or left, right is port when looking astern.

Lines for Course Alterations
When there is a planned course alteration it is convenient to use a single pre-planned position line to ensure that the course alteration is made in the right place (Fig 4.10, overleaf).

It is important that the mark used should give a position line as nearly as possible parallel to the new course. There is a temptation to select a mark

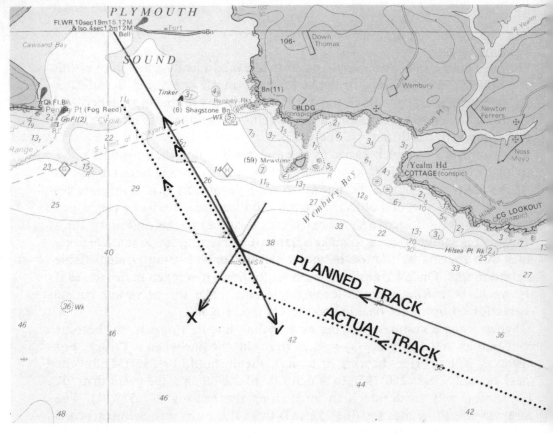

Fig 4.10 Examples of a good and bad bearing for the turning point

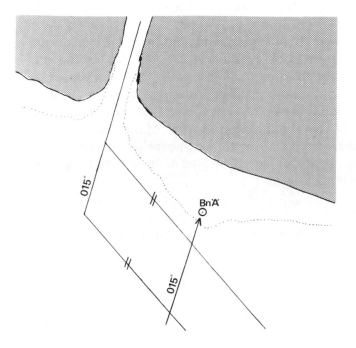

Fig 4.11 The use of a single, pre-planned position line

which is abeam on the old course because this gives the fastest possible rate of change of bearing and therefore apparent accuracy. The accuracy is fallacious. If the yacht is to port or starboard of her original track, turning on a position line nearly parallel to the new track will cause her to turn very close to the new track. A mark on the beam does not have this effect and is therefore useful as a turning mark only if the yacht is exactly on her original planned track.

Single Transferred Position Lines
It is possible to use a transferred position line to give the initial lead through a channel or into a harbour, although of course the transferred line does not give the same check on progress as a normal leading line. In Fig 4.11 a yacht is heading for a low-lying harbour entrance in poor visibility. The distance off the coast is not known precisely, but it is possible to note the time at which beacon A bears 015°(M), the heading into the river estuary. It is then a matter of running the distance through the water to the river entrance and turning on to the course of 015°(M).

The transferred position line can, of course, give the time only to turn towards the entrance, and the accuracy of the method depends upon the run between taking the bearing and turning on to the bearing being fairly short and the set and drift of the tidal stream being accurately known.

Clearing Lines
Clearing Bearings
Clearing lines are used to check that the yacht is not standing dangerously close to hazards. Fig 4.12 (overleaf) shows typical pre-planned clearing lines for the entrance to Wembury Bay. Provided that St Wemburgh's Church bears no more than 050°(M) she is clearing the Outer Slimers, and if it bears no less than 010°(M) she is clearing Western Ebb Rock. Clearing lines of that type are particularly useful when beating into a bay or harbour entrance as they allow the navigator to check that he is in safe water by watching a single bearing. He is, in fact, using a safe sector rather than a single bearing on a leading mark to make his approach.

Even if there is a well-defined leading line, it is worth planning clearing bearings as well. It is impossible to stay exactly on a leading line sailing to windward. With a leading wind or when motoring, it may be necessary to leave the leading line to keep clear of other vessels. With clearing lines pre-planned, the navigator knows precisely the limits within which he can sail and does not have to guess the amount by which it is safe to depart from the planned track.

In areas such as the Channel Islands where there are many unmarked hazards, a series of clearing lines, usually transits rather than compass bearings, allows passages to be made in safety through waters which appear

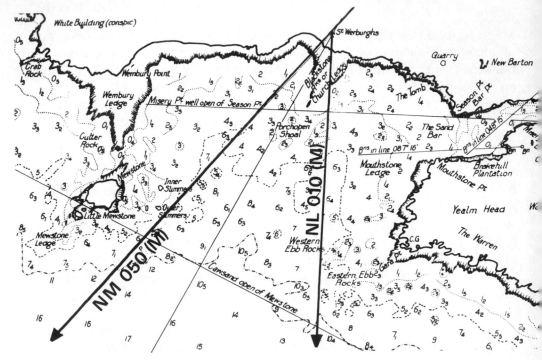

Fig 4.12 Clearing lines for the approach to Wembury Bay

from the chart to be strewn with rocks. Careful study of the chart usually shows which transits are likely to be helpful and they do not have to be exactly aligned marks. One rock open its own width left or right of another can be judged both visually and on the chart, and serves adequately to indicate that a danger has been passed and that it is clear to alter course on to the next heading.

Many lighthouses provide instant clearing bearings by night through the use of coloured sectors or a coloured sector light additional to the main light which shows only on a dangerous bearing. Fig 4.13 shows the leading light for Dartmouth Harbour. The white sector is the safe approach bearing, the red and green indicating its limits. Unfortunately, there is no convention by which red indicates always the port side of the channel and green the starboard. The significance of the colours appears to be decided according to the whim of the harbour authority rather than anything more logical.

Clearance by Sounding

Clearing lines do not have to be bearings or transits as soundings can often be used to give a safe clearing line. They are particularly useful when tacking along an evenly shelving shore or edge of a sandbank. Using soundings to keep in safe water requires more thought than simply deciding to tack out into deep water whenever the depth shoals to, say, 3m (10ft). Fig 4.14 shows a situation in which this would be fatal. The yacht would be perfectly safe

92

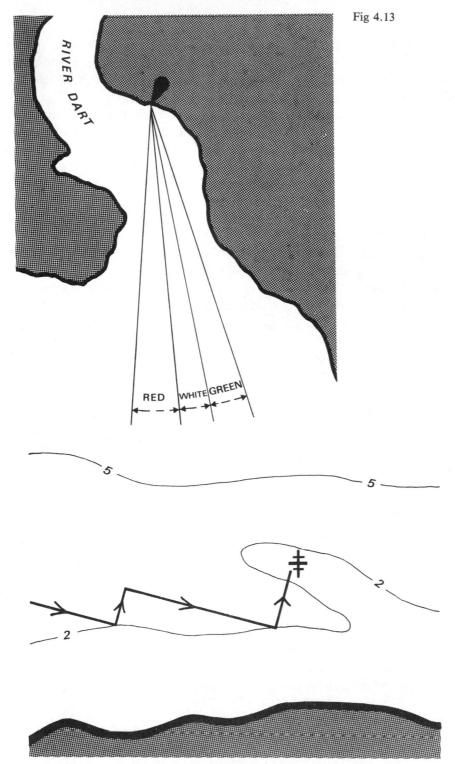

Fig 4.13

RIVER DART

RED WHITE GREEN

Fig 4.14 The wrong use of a depth contour line as a clearing line

until she reached the indentation in the shoal at A, but she would then stand into the indentation, tack and run aground. Traps for the unwary abound, but they can usually be avoided by close study of the chart and the selection of a safe depth contour as the clearing line.

Whether soundings or visual lines are used to give clearance, it is important to make sure that they really are clearing and not striking lines. If there is a rock a few yards on the shoal side of a depth-contour line, that contour is not a safe clearing line. Compass bearings should be selected so that at the very least they pass 2° from the danger from which they are designed to give clearance.

Choice of Method of Navigation

In this chapter we have looked at three navigational techniques: the use of position fixes, leading lines and clearing lines. Ideally, the navigator uses all three, a leading line to keep the yacht on track, with regular position fixes to check progress and guard against gross errors such as the misidentification of the leading mark, and he has pre-planned clearing lines available to define the limits of safe navigation should he have to leave the leading line. In practice, the geography of the coastline and the time available for navigation will seldom allow such meticulous attention to the yacht's position.

A three position line fix is the most reliable way to establish the position of a yacht at sea. A leading line establishes position only in one direction, but if that is the most important direction the speed and simplicity of use of a leading line may make it more appropriate than a fix. Similarly, a clearing line only shows that the yacht is in safe water, but again it is quick and easy to use.

At sea, well clear of dangers, position fixing allows the navigator to keep track of his position. He is likely to have plenty of time to navigate and decisions on course alterations are unlikely to have to be made in a hurry. Closer inshore, a leading line allows much more rapid appreciation of any tendency for the yacht to be set off track. When no suitable leading line is available or it is impossible to follow a leading line, clearing lines give a quick check on ultimate navigational safety.

The nearest ground to a yacht, unless she is in an alongside berth, is nearly always the sea bed. A depth by echo-sounder will seldom provide a position to plot on the chart, but it will very often warn the navigator when something has gone wrong with the navigation. Accurate position fixing is a good ideal, but an unquestioning faith in the accuracy of fixes is a prelude to disaster.

5 Tides and Tidal Streams

The vertical and horizontal movements of the sea surface owing to tidal effects are among the most important factors to be considered by the yachtsman making coastal and offshore passages. A knowledge of tidal movement and methods of calculation is essential if the tidal streams are to be used to advantage and tidal height restrictions avoided.

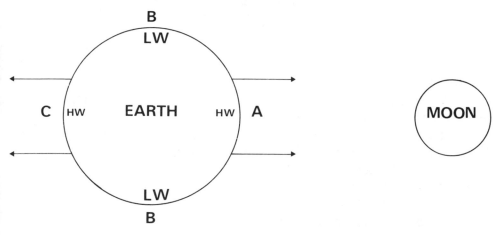

Fig 5.1 The tide-raising effect of the Moon

Causes of Tides

The periodic rise and fall of the sea surface and consequent tidal streams are caused by the gravitational attractions of the Sun and Moon. The Moon, being closer to the Earth, has an attractive force over twice that of the Sun. Fig 5.1 shows an imaginary Earth covered with water and with the Moon at some point in its orbit. The tide-raising forces of the Moon are causing high water at A, where the water is being 'pulled up' under the Moon and at C where it is being 'thrown out' as the Earth and Moon rotate about their common axis. As the Earth rotates, these 'waves' pass around its circumference causing successive high and low waters.

At new and full Moon, the Sun's attraction complements that of the Moon and tides of maximum range, spring tides, occur (Fig 5.2, overleaf).

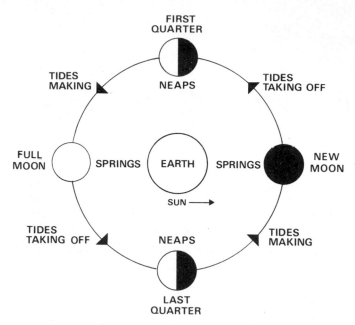

Fig 5.2 The combined tide-raising effects of the Sun and Moon

The Moon apparently passes around the Earth approximately every 24 hours 50 minutes. Therefore the interval between successive high waters is approximately 12 hours 25 minutes.

Greater than average spring tides occur when the Moon is closest to the Earth (at perigee), particularly when this occurs near the equinoxes (21 March and 23 September).

High waters at spring tides always occur at about the same time of day in any particular port. In the Solent, for instance, high waters at springs occur around midday and midnight, and high waters at neaps occur in the early morning and evening. In Plymouth, high water at springs are morning and evening and at neaps at about midday and midnight.

The geography of the Earth has a considerable influence upon the pattern of the tides experienced in different regions. Every ocean and sea, depending upon its size and depth, responds to the tide-raising forces with its own natural period of oscillation. In the Pacific Ocean, the period is approximately 25 hours and the tides are generally of a diurnal nature, one high and one low water every day. In the Atlantic Ocean the period is approximately 12½ hours and the tides are semi-diurnal or twice daily.

The tidal waves set up by these oscillations are only a metre of so in height in mid-ocean, but, as they reach the shallower waters around the continents, they increase in height and ranges in excess of 12m may occur. The shape of the tidal wave can also change owing to the effect of shallow water, often giving a longer period of ebb tide than flood.

Shallow-water effects also give rise to such tidal anomalies as the double high waters experienced in the Solent area. A bore is another example of shallow-water effect and is caused by a spring tide moving rapidly up a narrow channel or river as a wall of water, often a few metres high.

Meteorological Effects on the Tides

The pressure of the atmosphere can cause the level of the sea surface to vary from normal. Predictions are tabulated for average atmospheric pressure, but a change in pressure from the average by 34 millibars can alter the height of tide by as much as 0·3m.

Strong winds blowing over the sea can cause the water to build up and raise the sea-level on a lee shore. Strong winds blowing along a coastline, particularly with the rapid passage of a depression, can set up waves which will raise the predicted level of the water. When these waves coincide with spring tides, serious flooding may result.

Small oscillations in the level of the sea surface called seiches can be caused by the passage of a depression or line squall.

The level of the sea surface often varies from the levels predicted and tabulated in the tide tables. An adequate clearance must therefore be allowed over critical heights, particularly under abnormal conditions.

Tidal Levels and Datums

There are a number of terms used to describe tidal phenomena which have specific meanings (Fig 5.3, overleaf).

Chart Datum The level to which soundings and drying heights are referred on the chart and above which heights of tide are given in the tide tables. The level of chart datum generally coincides with the level of lowest astronomical tide (LAT). This is the lowest level to which the tide can be expected to fall under average meteorological conditions and under any combination of astronomical conditions.

Mean High Water Springs (MHWS); Mean Low Water Springs (MLWS) These are the average heights of high water and low water at spring tides. The charted heights of terrestrial objects (lights, peaks, bridges, etc) are referred to the level of mean high water springs.

Mean High Water Neaps (MHWN); Mean Low Water Neaps (MLWN) These are the average heights of high water and low water at neap tides.

Mean Tide Level This is the average value of all heights of high and low water over a period. This level does not always coincide with mean sea-level, but both terms are often referred to as mean level. Ordnance Datum (Newlyn) is the land reference level and corresponds to the average value of mean sea-level at Newlyn during 1915–21.

Height of Tide The vertical distance between chart datum and the sea level.

Spring Range The difference in height between MHWS and MLWS.

Neap Range The difference in height between MHWN and MLWN.

Charted Sounding The depth to the sea bed below chart datum level.

Drying Height The heights above chart datum of features which are periodically covered and uncovered by the tides.

High Water (HW) The highest level reached by the tide in one tidal oscillation.

Low Water (LW) The lowest level reached by the tide in one tidal oscillation.

Range of the Tide The vertical difference in height between successive high and low waters.

Duration of the Tide The interval in time between successive high and low waters.

Interval from High Water The interval in time between a given time and the nearest high water. Either − (before) or + (after) high-water time.

Rise The vertical difference between the low-water height and the water level.

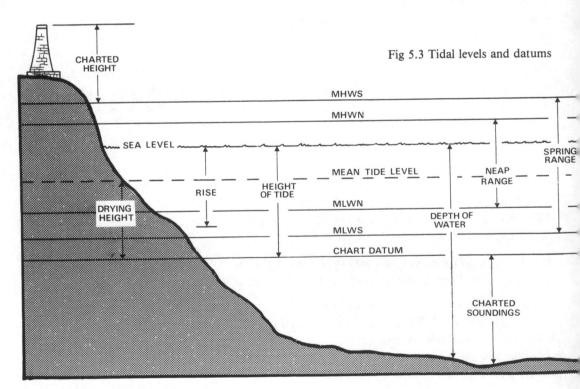

Fig 5.3 Tidal levels and datums

Tide Tables

Tide tables provide daily predictions of the times and heights of high and low water at a number of standard ports. Time and height differences from the standard port are provided also for a number of secondary ports in the area. Secondary ports are normally in the vicinity of the standard port, but this is not always the case, the main criterion being that the secondary port has a similar tidal curve to the standard port.

The following tide tables are in general use:

1   *Admiralty Tide Tables* (*ATT*), Vol I, European waters. (Other volumes of *ATT* are: Vol II, Atlantic and Indian Oceans and Vol III, Pacific Ocean and adjacent seas.)
2   *Reed's Nautical Almanac* The tables are designed for the use of yachtsmen who cruise in European waters. *Reed's* contains much other information of general use as well as tide tables.
3   *Other Almanacs* Although *Reed's* has been the accepted yachtsman's almanac for many years, there are now a number of choices. Most of them use a form of tide tables similar in layout to the Admiralty's.
4   *Local Tide Tables* These are printed by or on behalf of local ports and harbours for distribution to the local shipping and yachting communities.

Calculations

The yachtsman's cruising grounds include many small harbours and estuaries around coasts where tidal ranges are large and tidal streams are strong. He requires accurate tidal information that will enable him to enter and depart safely with adequate clearance over shoals and drying banks. Only by making accurate tidal calculations can a determinable margin of clearance be allowed or estimated. For this reason the calculations in this book are carried out by the Admiralty methods, as these are the most accurate generally available to the yachtsman.

The method of tidal predication used in the Admiralty tide table is based on tidal curves, a graphic representation of the way in which the tide rises and falls. This method is easier to understand than the strictly numerical tables in *Reed's Nautical Almanac*. As *Reed's* contains so much information in a single volume, it is more widely used in yachts than is the Admiralty tide table, but anyone who has learnt tidal calculations by the Admiralty method is likely to have a good understanding of the subject and be able to switch to any other form of tide table without difficulty.

The twelfths rule is also included as this provides a simple method of finding approximate times and heights of tide.

Admiralty Tide Tables (Vol I, European Waters)

Part I of the tables gives daily predictions of the times and heights of high and low water at a number of selected standard ports. Included with each set of predictions is a diagram illustrating the tidal curve at springs and at neaps.

99

Part II of the tables gives time and height differences to the standard port for a number of secondary ports in the area which have similar tidal curves. An introductory section describes the methods used to predict tidal information and the effect of meteorological conditions on these predictions. Supplementary information is provided on the Solent tides, conversion tables from feet to metres and vice versa, and also details of tidal levels at standard ports.

The tables also give details of the harmonic tidal constants for secondary ports. These allow the tidal curve to be constructed. This enables very accurate predictions to be made for secondary ports, but the work involved is time-consuming and unlikely to be justified for the purposes of yacht navigation.

Finding Times and Heights of High and Low Water
Standard Ports
All predicted times are given in the standard time of the port. In the case of the UK this is Greenwich Mean Time (GMT). During British Summer Time (BST) 1 hour should be added to the tabulated time to convert to the time in use. The zone time used is shown at the top of each page and the sign indicates how the zone correction should be applied to the local time to find GMT. Heights of tide are given in metres.

The required times and heights are easily lifted from the tables, with a little care to make sure that the right day and month are used.

Secondary Ports
Time and height differences to apply to the standard ports are found in Part II of the tables. Each secondary port is allocated an *Admiralty Tide Table* number which is indexed for easy reference. Time differences vary with the times of high and low water at the standard port and height differences vary with heights of high and low water. A certain amount of interpolation or even extrapolation is therefore necessary to obtain accurate results. This interpolation may appear complicated to the non-mathematical because there is quite an array of figures involved. As with all mathematical processes, it is 'easy when you know how' and finding out how calls for practice.

NP204 is a useful pro-forma for tidal calculations produced by the Admiralty and available from chart agents. The following examples illustrate the procedure.

Find the times and heights of high and low water at Braye (Alderney) on 16 August: the index shows that Braye is number 1603, and, looking this up in the secondary ports, the standard port is St Helier. The information available in the tide table is shown in the upper part of Table 5.1.

Using NP204 the calculation of the required times and heights is:

CHANNEL ISLANDS - ST. HELIER

AUGUST

	TIME	M
16	0345	2.3
	0927	9.8
SA	1556	2.5
	2139	9.8

No.	PLACE	Lat. N.	Long. E.	TIME DIFFERENCES High Water	TIME DIFFERENCES Low Water (Zone −0100)	HEIGHT DIFFERENCES (IN METRES) MHWS	MHWN	MLWN	MLWS
05	ST. HELIER . . . (see page 222)			0900 and 2100	0300 and 1500	0200 and 1400	0900 and 2100	11·1	8·1	4·1	1·3

(Zone G.M.T.)

No.	PLACE	Lat. N.	Long. E.	HW	LW	HW	LW	MHWS	MHWN	MLWN	MLWS
03	*Alderney* Braye	49 43	2 12	+0040	+0050	+0025	+0105	−4·8	−3·4	−1·5	−0·5

TIDAL PREDICTION FORM

STANDARD PORT *ST. HELIER* ....TIME or HEIGHT REQUIRED...............

SECONDARY PORT *BRAYE* ....DATE *16 AUGUST* TIME ZONE *GMT* ....

	TIME		HEIGHT	
	HW	LW	HW	LW
STANDARD PORT	1 *0927*	2 *0345*	3 *9.8m*	4 *2.3m*
Seasonal Changes in ML	− Standard Port		5	
	+ Secondary Port		6	
DIFFERENCES	7 *+0041*	8 *+0035*	9 *−4.2m*	10 *−0.9m*
SECONDARY PORT	11 *1008*	12 *0420*	13 *5.6m*	14 *1.4m*
DURATION	15	RANGE(a)St (b)Sec	16(a)	16(b)

Table 5.1

Boxes 1–4 are completed by extracting the times and heights shown in the tide table for the standard port. GMT is used because the time corrections are related to GMT.

Boxes 5 and 6 are ignored. Seasonal changes in mean level are so small in most cases that, for all practical purposes, it is not worth bothering about them.

Boxes 7–10 are completed by interpolating between the figures given. The LW time correction is a good example of the type of interpolation required.

The table shows that for a LW time of 0200 the correction is +0025 and for a LW time of 0900 the correction is +0105. The time of LW on this particular occasion, 0345, is somewhere between the two.

Expanding the table to show the time intervals involved gives:

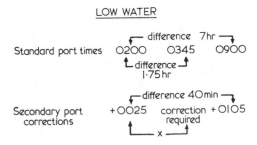

The table is now slightly simplified. The LW times either side of today's LW time have been extracted as these are the times on which to work.

To find the correction for today's LW it is necessary to find x. By simple proportion:

$$\frac{1 \cdot 75}{7} = \frac{x}{40}$$

$$or,\ x = \frac{1 \cdot 75}{7} \times 40$$

$$ie,\ x = 10$$

Returning to the expanded tabulation and applying x, the time correction required is +0025 + 10 = +0035. Similarly, the height correction table can be expanded to show the height intervals, this time taking HW as an example:

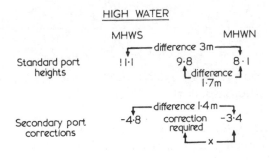

Again the requirement is to find a value for x, and by simple proportion:

$$\frac{1\cdot7}{3}=\frac{x}{1\cdot4}$$

$$or,\ x=\frac{1\cdot7}{3}\times1\cdot4$$

$$ie,\ x=0\cdot8$$

Returning to the expanded table and applying x, the height correction is $-3\cdot4-0\cdot8=-4\cdot2$.

Finally, the times can be converted to BST to give HW 1108, $5\cdot6$M, LW 0520, $1\cdot4$M.

It might appear simpler to convert to BST at the start of the calculation, but this would introduce an inaccuracy as the time differences at the secondary port are related to times of HW and LW given in GMT.

The same interpolation calculations can be shown graphically by plotting, for time of LW, times of low water at the standard port against time corrections. The relationship is linear so the two known points on the graph can be plotted, joined with a straight line, and any intermediate point read off (Fig 5.4).

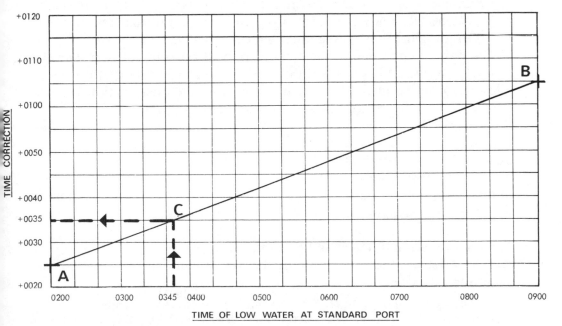

Fig 5.4 Interpolation for differences in time corrections

103

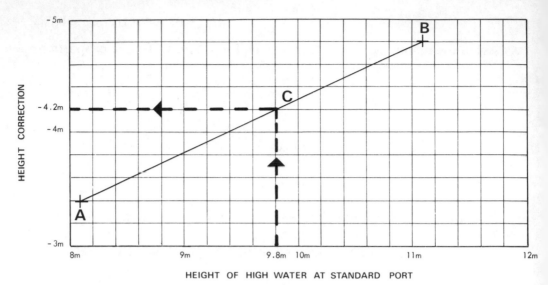

Fig 5.5 Interpolation for differences in height corrections

The height correction graph can be drawn in exactly the same way (Fig 5.5). Drawing graphs for these relatively simple problems is a rather laborious way to make the interpolations unless a number of calculations for the same secondary port are likely to be made. The real advantage of drawing the graph, for some people, is that it enables them to understand the calculations in a way which they would never do if just working with numbers.

Returning to the main calculation, the figures in boxes 11–14 are found by applying the secondary port corrections (differences) to the standard port times and heights. Finally, the times are converted to BST.

The only complication in these calculations is the interpolation, and the example just worked shows that there may be a significant difference to be allowed for in the interpolations. In many cases the interpolation is much simpler and can be carried out by eye without any loss of accuracy. When an approximate time or height of high or low water is needed, as is very often the case, a sufficiently accurate figure can be estimated without going through the full mathematical procedure of interpolation. The errors which are likely to arise from an estimation are unlikely to be more than 5 minutes in time or 0·2m in height, and these are likely to be insignificant compared with the safety margin which must in any case be allowed.

Finding Intermediate Times and Heights

All the tidal problems confronting the yachtsman fall into one of the following categories:

1 Finding the limiting times between which it is possible to enter or leave a harbour. This may involve a berth which dries out or a limiting depth over a bar.

2   Finding the reduction to a sounding in order to make a comparison with the charted depth.
3   Finding the minimum depth in which to anchor to provide adequate clearance at low water.
4   Finding the time when there will be adequate clearance under a bridge.

Each of these problems involves one of two calculations:
  a Finding the height of tide at a given time between high and low water;
or b finding the time at which the tide reaches a given height between high and low water.

Thus, there are only two calculations which have to be carried out, but these may present themselves in a number of different disguises. It is therefore necessary to rearrange the figures with which one is presented to reduce the problem to one of the two basic calculations. The rearrangement involves relating to the problem to chart datum.

Example 5.1
What height of tide is required to give a yacht drawing 1·5m a clearance of 1m over a bank with a charted depth of 1·2m?

Draught	1·5m
Clearance	1·0m
Depth required	2·5m
Charted depth	1·2m
Height of tide	1·3m

(Fig 5.6)

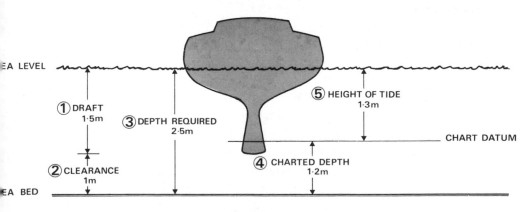

Fig 5.6

105

Example 5.2

What height of tide is required to give a yacht drawing 2m a clearance of 1m over a sandbank charted as drying 1·4m?

Draught	2·0m
Clearance	1·0m
Sandbank	1·4m
Height of tide	4·4m
(Fig 5.7)	

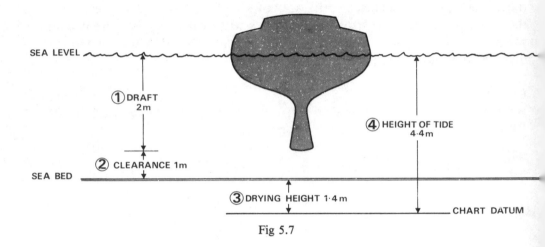

Fig 5.7

Example 5.3

The echo-sounder records a depth of 18m. If the height of tide is 3·5m, what is the reduced sounding to compare with the charted depth? Draft 2·5m and distance from the keel to the transducer is 1·2m.

Draught	2·5m
Transducer/keel	1·2m
Trans/water line	1·3m
Sounding	18·0m
Depth of water	19·3m
Height of tide	3·5m
Reduced soundings	15·8m
(Fig 5.8)	

106

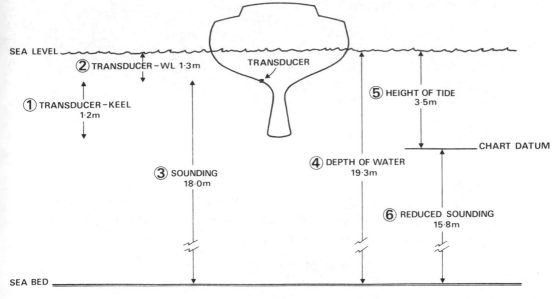

Fig 5.8

Example 5.4

A sounding of 10m was obtained by lead line on anchoring when the height of tide was calculated to be 5·5m. What will be the clearance under the keel at low water if the height of tide at low water is 1·2m and the draft of the vessel is 2·5m?

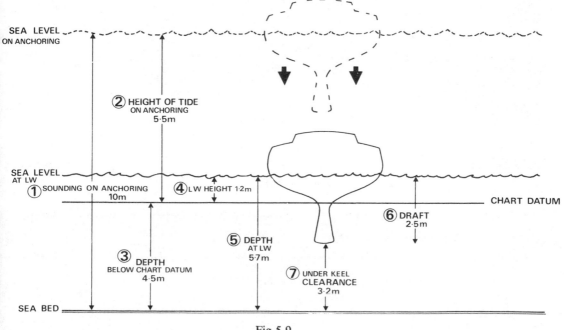

Fig 5.9

Sounding	10m
Height of tide	5·5m
Depth to chart datum	4·5m
Height of low water	1·2m
Depth of low water	5·7m
Draught	2·5m
Under keel clearance	3·2m

(Fig 5.9)

Example 5.5

The charted height of a lighthouse is 20m. What is the correction to apply to this charted height to give the height of the light above sea-level? Height of tide is 1·5m and height of MHWS is 5·3m.

Height of MHWS	5·3m
Height of tide	1·5m
MHWS above sea-level	3·8m
Charted height of light	20·0m
Height of light above SL	23·8m

(Fig 5.10)

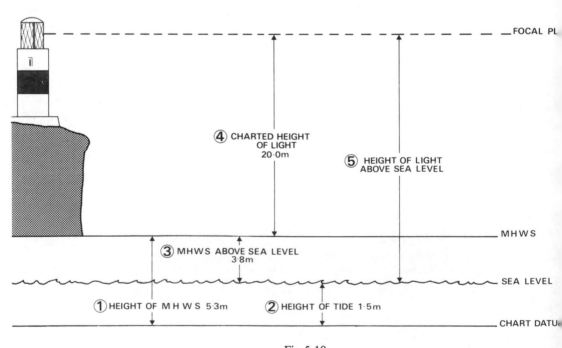

Fig 5.10

108

Example 5.6

The charted height of a bridge is 17·9m. What is the masthead clearance for a yacht with a masthead height of 18·8m above the waterline when the height of tide is 6m? MHWS is 7·3m above CD.

Masthead to waterline	18·8m
Height of MHWS	7·3m
Height of tide	6·0m
Correction to height	1·3m
Charted height bridge	17·9m
Bridge to sea-level	19·2m
Masthead to sea-level	18·8m
Masthead clearance	0·4m
(Fig 5.11)	

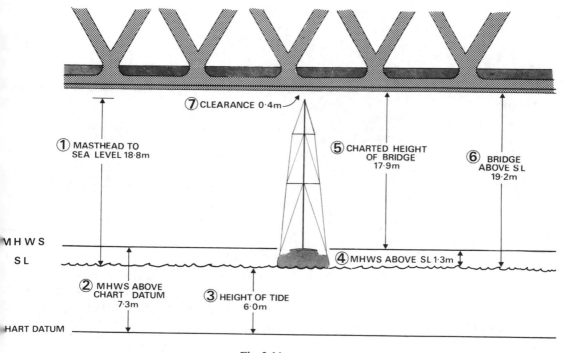

Fig 5.11

Example 5.7

What is the depth by echo-sounder in which to anchor to give a clearance of 2m at low water? The distance from the transducer to the waterline is 1m and the vessel's draft is 2·6m. The calculated height of tide when anchoring is 2·5m and the height of low water is 0·5m.

Draught	2·6m
Clearance required	2·0m
Depth required at LW	4·6m
Height of tide when anchoring	2·5m
Height of low water	0·5m
Tide to fall	2·0m
Depth required at low water	4·6m
Fall of tide to low water	2·0m
Total depth of water required	6·6m
Transducer below waterline	1·0m
Depth required by echo-sounder	5·6m

(Fig 5.12)

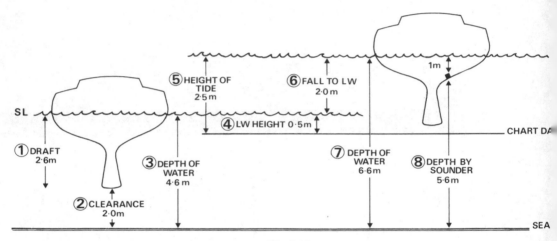

Fig 5.12

The Rule of Twelfths

The rule of twelfths is a simple method of predicting the approximate height of tide at times between high and low water. It assumes that the tidal curve is symmetrical and that the duration of rise or fall is approximately 6 hours. It is therefore useless in areas such as the Solent where neither of these conditions applies.

The rule states:

During the first hour the ride rises/falls by $\frac{1}{12}$ the range
During the second hour the tide rises/falls by $\frac{2}{12}$ the range
During the third hour the tide rises/falls by $\frac{3}{12}$ the range
During the fourth hour the tide rises/falls by $\frac{3}{12}$ the range
During the fifth hour the tide rises/falls by $\frac{2}{12}$ the range
During the sixth hour the tide rises/falls by $\frac{1}{12}$ the range
(Fig 5.13)

110

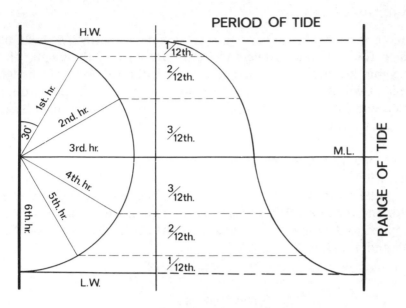

RISE AND FALL OF TIDE

Fig 5.13 The derivation of the rule of twelfths

The rule can be stated more simply by applying it only to the 3 hours either side of high or low water:

In the hour before or after HW or LW the tide rises or falls by $\frac{1}{12}$ the range.
In the 2 hours before or after HW or LW the tide rises or falls by ¼ the range
In the 3 hours before or after HW or LW the tide rises or falls by ½ the range.

The rule, in either form, is an approximation and must be used as such.

Example 5.8
What will be the height of tide at Dover at 1600 BST on 1 July?

ENGLAND, SOUTH COAST

DOVER

	JULY	
	TIME	M
1	0032	6·5
	0806	0·9
TU	1259	6·6
	2029	0·9

High water is at 1359, BST, 6·6m and the range is 5·7m. Fall in 2 hours is ¼ × 5·7 = 1·4m.
Height of tide at 1600 BST is about 5·2m.

111

The method is only intended to give approximate answers, so it should not be used to find accurate answers to tidal questions. If the height of tide 2 hours 35 minutes after low water is required, the rule of twelfths will not provide it. It will give, however, approximate heights for 2 and 3 hours after low water and these approximations, in some circumstances, may be all that the navigator needs to know.

Height of Tide by Admiralty Tide Tables

The predictions for each standard port include a graph (Fig 5.14) showing the mean tidal curve at springs and at neaps. The arguments for the graph are the factor and the interval from high water. The factor is a multiplier which, when applied to the range of the tide, gives the rise of tide. Thus the factor is 0 at LW and 1 at HW.

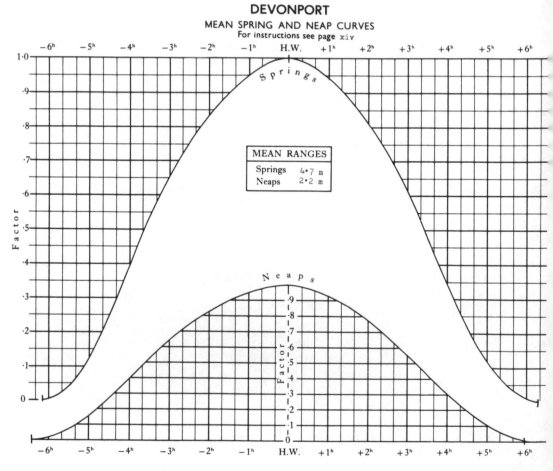

Fig 5.14

$$\text{Factor} = \frac{\text{Rise of tide}}{\text{Range}}$$

or
$$\text{Rise of tide} = \text{Factor} \times \text{Range}$$

For example, if the height of tide is required 3 hours before HW between a LW height of 0·3m and a HW height of 5·0m:

> Range = 5·0 − 0·3 = 4·7m (Springs)
> Factor from the curve for 3 hours before is 0·65
> Therefore: Rise = Range × Factor
>   = 4·7 × 0·65 = 3·1m
> Added to the LW height gives a height of tide
> equal to 0·3 + 3·1 = 4·4m

When the range of the tide for the day is more than, or close to, the spring range, the factor is found from the spring curve. If the range is less than, or close to, the neap range, the factor is found from the neap curve. When the range is between springs and neaps interpolation is required. NP204 provides a convenient method for working.

Example 5.9
What will be the height of tide at Devonport at 1000 BST on Wednesday 16 April? The relevant section of the tide table shows:

DEVONPORT

APRIL

	TIME	M
16 W	0022	0·2
	0646	5·9
	1245	0·2
	1910	5·8

The calculation, using NP204, is shown overleaf. The only part of the calculation which requires any explanation is boxes 20 and 21. The factor in box 20 is found from the tidal curve for Devonport (Fig 5.14). The range is greater than the mean spring range, so the spring curve is used. For the multiplication of range and factor to give the rise there is a multiplication table in the front of the *Admiralty Tide Table*. Many people find that long multiplication or a hand-held calculator give as quick and accurate an answer.

113

TIDAL PREDICTION FORM

STANDARD PORT *DEVONPORT*......TIME or HEIGHT REQUIRED...*AT 1000 BST (0900 GMT)*

SECONDARY PORT ....DATE *13 APRIL*...TIME ZONE *GMT*.......

	TIME		HEIGHT	
	HW	LW	HW	LW
STANDARD PORT	1 *06 46*	2 –	3 *5.9m*	4 *0.2m*
Seasonal Changes in ML	− Standard Port		5	
	+ Secondary Port		6	
DIFFERENCES	7 –	8 –	9 –	10 –
SECONDARY PORT	11 –	12 –	13 –	14 –
DURATION	15 –	RANGE(a)St (b)Sec	16(a) *5.7m*	16(b) –

*Springs/Neaps/Interpolate

START— Height at Given Time

REQUIRED TIME	17 *0900*
TIME HW	18 *06 46*
INTERVAL	19 *+0214*

FACTOR	20 *0.77*

RISE	21 *0.77* ✗ *5.7 = 4.4*
HEIGHT LW	22 *0.2*
HEIGHT REQUIRED	23 *4.6m*

START— Time for Given Height

*Delete as necessary

Table 5.2

Example 5.10

What will be the height of tide at St Mary's, Isles of Scilly, at 1400 BST on Wednesday 9 April? The information to be extracted from the tide tables is shown in Table 5.2. In this example the calculation is slightly more complicated because the time of HW and heights of HW and LW must be calculated. Once this has been done, the calculation is exactly the same as for a standard port.

114

DEVONPORT

APRIL

9
W

0509	2.0
1111	4.3
1746	2.1
2354	4.5

No.	PLACE	Lat. N.	Long. W.	TIME DIFFERENCES High Water Low Water (Zone G.M.T.)				HEIGHT DIFFERENCES (IN METRES) MHWS MHWN MLWN MLWS			
14	DEVONPORT · ·	(see page 2)		0000 and 1200	0600 and 1800	0000 and 1200	0600 and 1800	5·5	4·4	2·2	0·8
1	*Isles of Scilly* St. Mary's · · ·	49 55	6 19	−0030	−0110	−0100	−0020	+0·2	−0·1	−0·2	−0·1

TIDAL PREDICTION FORM

STANDARD PORT *DEVONPORT*............TIME or HEIGHT REQUIRED. *AT 1400 BST (1300 GMT)*.

SECONDARY PORT *ST. MARY'S*....DATE *9 APRIL*...TIME ZONE..*GMT*......

	TIME			HEIGHT		
	HW		LW	HW		LW
STANDARD PORT	1 *1111*	2	−	3 *4.3*	4	*2.1*
Seasonal Changes in ML	− Standard Port			5		
	+ Secondary Port			6		
DIFFERENCES	7 *−0035*	8	−	9 *−0.1*	10	*−0.2*
SECONDARY PORT	11 *1036*	12	−	13 *4.2*	14	*1.9*
DURATION	15 −	RANGE(a)St (b)Sec		16(a) *2.2*		16(b) *2.3*

*Springs/Neaps/Interpolate

START—
Height at
Given Time ⬇

REQUIRED TIME	17	*1300*
TIME HW	18	*1036*
INTERVAL	19	*+0224*

FACTOR	20	*0.68*

RISE	21	*1.6m*
HEIGHT LW	22	*1.9m*
HEIGHT REQUIRED	23	*3.5m*

⬆ START—
Time for
Given Height

*Delete as necessary   Table 5.3

In boxes 16(a) and (b) of Table 5.3, ranges for both the standard and secondary port are shown. The range at the standard port is used to determine whether the spring or neap curve should be used, the range at the secondary port is multiplied by the factor to give the height of the tide. In this example there is not much difference, but that is by no means always the case.

The preceding examples illustrate finding the height of tide at a particular time. Other situations involve finding the time at which the tide reaches a particular height.

Example 5.11 (see Table 5.4, p118)
At what time in daylight on Sunday 6 April will the tide first reach a height of 7m at St Helier? The data in the tide table is:

ST HELIER

APRIL

	TIME	M
6 SU	0349	2·7
	0924	9·6
	1559	3·0
	2142	9·4

The tidal curve for St Helier is shown in Fig 5.15. In this type of calculation the order of working boxes 17–23 is reversed. A simple interpolation is required between the spring and neap curves for the interval in box 19.

Example 5.12 (see Table 5.5, p119)
At what time in daylight on Saturday 19 April will the tide first reach a height of 4m at Braye? The data required from the tide table is shown in Table 5.1 (page 101) and the actual predictions for the standard port are:

ST HELIER

APRIL

	TIME	M
19 SA	0338	1·5
	0910	10·6
	1556	1·9
	2125	10·2

In this example the range at the standard port is sufficiently close to springs for no interpolation to be required.

ST. HELIER

MEAN SPRING AND NEAP CURVES
For instructions see page xiv

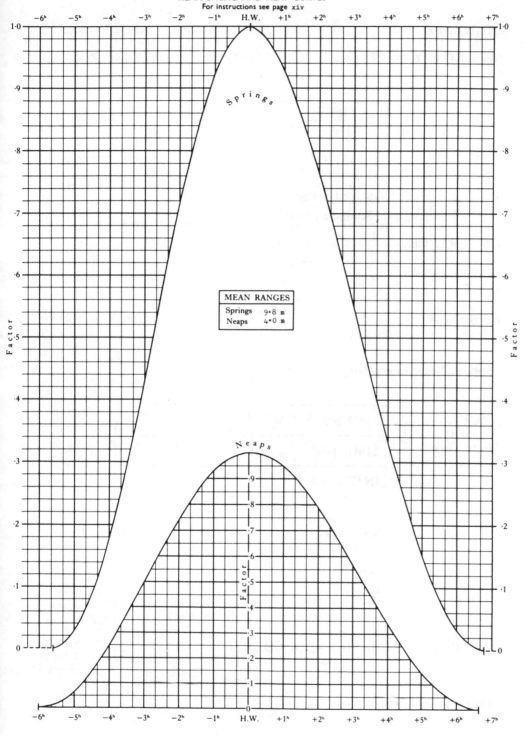

MEAN RANGES

Springs	9·8 m
Neaps	4·0 m

Fig 5.15

TIDAL PREDICTION FORM

STANDARD PORT ...*ST. HELIER*....TIME or HEIGHT REQUIRED.*FOR HT 7*

SECONDARY PORT ....DATE.*6 APRIL*...TIME ZONE..........

	TIME			HEIGHT		
	HW		LW	HW		LW
STANDARD PORT	1 *0924*	2	–	3 *9.6m*	4	*2.7m*
Seasonal Changes in ML	– Standard Port			5		
	+ Secondary Port			6		
DIFFERENCES	7 –	8	–	9 –	10	–
SECONDARY PORT	11 –	12	–	13 –	14	–
DURATION	15 –	RANGE(a)St (b)Sec		16(a) *6.9m*	16(b)	–

*Springs/Neaps/Interpolate

START— Height at Given Time

REQUIRED TIME	17	*0657 GMT*
TIME HW	18	*0924*
INTERVAL	19	*−02 27*

07 57 BST

FACTOR	20 *4.3 ÷ 6.9 = 0.62*

RISE	21	*4.3m*
HEIGHT LW	22	*2.7m*
HEIGHT REQUIRED	23	*7m*

START— Time for Given Height

*Delete as necessary

Table 5.4

118

TIDAL PREDICTION FORM

STANDARD PORT *ST. HELIER*......TIME or HEIGHT REQUIRED *AT WHICH HEIGHT WILL BE.. 4.m*......

SECONDARY PORT *BRAYE*...........DATE *19 APRIL*...TIME ZONE *GMT*.......

	TIME		HEIGHT	
	HW	LW	HW	LW
STANDARD PORT	1 *0910*	2 *-*	3 *10.6m*	4 *1.5m*
Seasonal Changes in ML	−Standard Port		5	
	+Secondary Port		6	
DIFFERENCES	7 *+00 40*	8 *-*	9 *-4.6m*	10 *-0.6*
SECONDARY PORT	11 *0950*	12 *-*	13 *6m*	14 *0.9m*
DURATION	15 *-*	RANGE(a)St (b)Sec	16(a) *9.1m*	16(b) *5.1m*

*Springs/Neaps/Interpolate

START—
Height at
Given Time ⌐↓

REQUIRED TIME	17 *0725* *GMT*
TIME HW	18 *0950*
INTERVAL	19 *-0225*

0825 BST

FACTOR	20 $\dfrac{3.1}{5.1} = 0.61$

RISE	21 *3.1m*
HEIGHT LW	22 *0.9m*
HEIGHT REQUIRED	23 *4m*

↑ START—
Time for
Given Height

Table 5.5

119

Tidal Calculations for the Solent

In the Solent area, between Poole and Chichester, the tidal curves are asymetric and there is considerable variation in the curves both between ports only a few miles apart and between springs and neaps. The *Admiralty Tide Tables* includes tidal curves for all the ports of any significance in this area, related to the range of tide at Portsmouth. At a number of these ports a double high water occurs and corrections for time and height for both high waters are given (Fig 5.16).

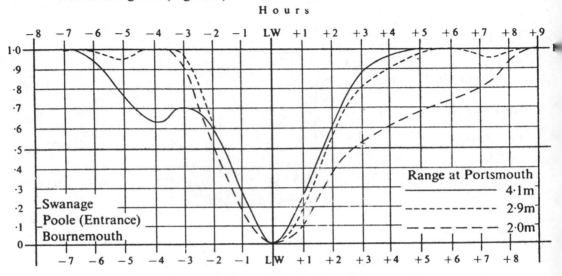

Fig 5.16 Tidal curves for Swanage—Bournemouth

Tidal Calculations in Practice

The practical significance of accurate tidal predictions depends very much upon the area. Where tidal ranges are large and where there are bars or shallow banks to cross, accurate predictions are essential. In areas where the tidal range is small and the majority of the harbours and their approaches carry deep water at all states of the tide, predictions are less important.

A useful practical way to deal with tidal calculations is to calculate times of high and low water for significant ports and draw a sketch of the tidal curve for the day, to conform to the shape of the curve for the standard port. This makes a quick approximation of the height available at any time and avoids the tedium of repeated recalculation.

Co-tidal and Co-range Charts

Co-tidal charts, which show places at which the times of high and low water are the same and co-range charts, which show places at which the range of the tide are the same, are published by the Hydrographic Department. These are particularly useful in the Thames Estuary, where it is often useful to be

120

able to calculate heights of tide over off-lying banks, many miles from any standard or secondary port.

Causes of Tidal Streams

A tidal stream is the periodic horizontal movement of the sea surface owing to the tide-raising forces of the Sun and Moon. The flood and ebb of the tidal streams around the coasts and up rivers result in the vertical movement of the sea surface which we call the tides. The tidal flow follows a similar pattern to the times of high and low water in the area. Where the tides are of semi-diurnal nature, the tidal stream will flood for about 6 hours and ebb for a similar period. Short periods of slack water will normally occur at the times of high and low water in the area, but this is not always the case.

Where the tidal stream flows along the coast the times at which the direction of the stream changes are unlikely to coincide with the times of local high and low water. The time of change of direction of the stream, however, is always related to the time of local high water or low water, the change of direction occurring the same number of hours before or after local high water each day.

Tidal streams are either rectilinear, flowing in approximately reciprocal directions, or rotary, changing direction clockwise or anti-clockwise through 360°. In either case, they should theoretically return to their starting positions after one tidal cycle of 12½ hours.

The yachtsman requires to know the direction and velocity of the tidal stream for any position and at any instant in time, to enable him to make due allowance when finding the course made good or the course to steer.

Terms Related to Tidal Streams

The following terms relate to surface movement:

Flood Tide A term applied both to the rising tide and to the direction of flow as the tide rises.

Ebb Tide A term applied both to the falling tide and to the direction of flow as the tide falls.

Slack Water A period of negligible horizontal water movement when a rectilinear tidal stream changes direction.

Current The horizontal movement of water owing to meteorological and oceanographical factors. It is normally constant in direction and rate although there may be seasonal fluctuations.

Surface Drift The movement of the surface water owing to wind effect.

Flow The total surface movement of the sea.

Set The direction in which a tidal stream or current is flowing.

121

Drift The distance a vessel is set under the influence of the tidal stream and current.

Eddy A deflection of the stream by an obstruction (island, headland, jetty, etc). It may take the form of a circular motion in the water or a movement of the water in a different direction from that of the tidal stream in the vicinity.

Race A fast-running stream caused by water flowing through a constricted channel or over shallows or by convergent streams, often found in the vicinity of headlands.

Overfalls A turbulent area of water caused by the tidal stream flowing over underwater obstructions or an uneven sea bed.

Sources of Tidal Stream Information
Information regarding tidal streams can be found on Admiralty charts, in tidal stream atlases and sailing directions.

Tidal Stream Atlases
This is the form of presentation of tidal stream information which is easiest to assimilate and use. Eight atlases are published by the Hydrographic Department, covering the UK coastal waters and the adjacent European coasts. *Yachtsmen's almanacs* include atlases for the same area. Each atlas contains a page showing the direction and rates at springs and neaps for each hour before and after high water at a standard port. Fig 5.17 shows a typical page.

The rates of the stream are given in tenths of knots, the first figure relates to neaps and the second to springs. Interpolation is required for rates between springs and neaps and a table is provided at the front of each atlas which makes this interpolation extremely simple. If an exact rate is required for a position between two given rates, it can be found by interpolation.

For easy reference, the times to which each chart refers can be marked in pencil at the top of the page. It is then very easy to study the effect the streams are likely to have during a passage and to extract information whenever it is required.

Charted Tidal Stream Information
Positions at which the tidal stream has been measured accurately are shown on charts as letters enclosed in diamonds. A table shows directions and rates for the position of each diamond for each hour before and after high water at a reference port (Fig 1.14, p28).

This type of presentation of tidal stream information is extremely accurate for the area to which it refers but, because of the wide spacing between diamonds, it is difficult and sometimes misleading to interpolate between

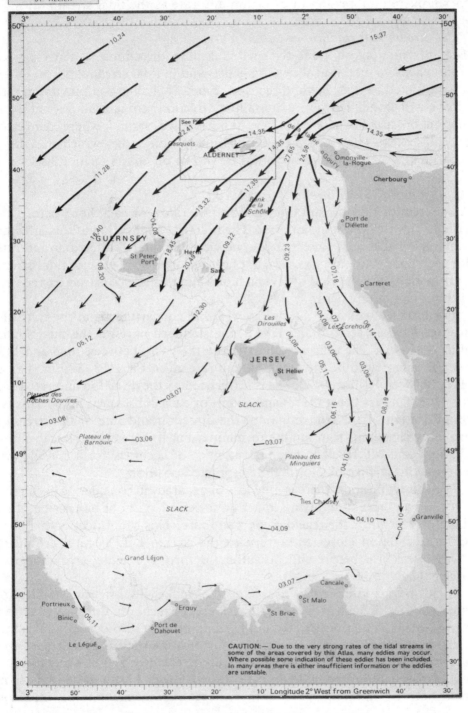

CAUTION:— Due to the very strong rates of the tidal streams in some of the areas covered by this Atlas, many eddies may occur. Where possible some indication of these eddies has been included. In many areas there is either insufficient information or the eddies are unstable.

Fig 5.17 An example from a tidal stream atlas

them. The tabular presentation of the information is not as easy to assimilate for an overall impression of direction and rate as the tidal stream atlas.

Tidal Stream Information in Sailing Directions

The information on tidal streams in sailing directions is generally less comprehensive than that shown on charts and in tidal stream atlases. Often, it is restricted to the general directions, times of change and maximum rates of ebb and flood. However, the sailing directions contain additional information on areas where rates are abnormally fast and where dangerous overfalls exist. They also provide information on eddies which may be of such limited extent that they cannot be shown on charts or in atlases.

Application of Tidal Stream Information

All sources of tidal stream information give rates for each hour before and after high water at a standard port. The practical application of this information may require some interpolation between the quoted directions and rates for each hour, but most practical applications involve the use of tidal stream information over a period of several hours and this can be extracted and used without any interpolation.

For instance, consider the case in which the departure fix at the start of a passage is taken at 1045 and HW at the standard port for the tidal stream atlas is at 1403. The tidal stream affecting the yacht between 1045 and 1130 may be assumed to be the direction and rate given for 1103, 3 hours before HW. Between 1130 and 1230 she is influenced by the direction and rate given for 1203, 2 hours before HW, and so on for each subsequent hour. This is a simplification of the true situation, the direction and rate of the stream is probably changing from minute to minute, but it is a very practical simplification, and will result in minimal sacrifice of accuracy for a considerable gain in convenience of plotting the estimated position.

For shorter periods, there is little loss of accuracy in considering each given direction and rate as applying to a 1 hour period, ½ hour either side of the time for which it is the true direction and rate. This simplification may be a misrepresentation close to the turn of the stream but, as rates are nearly always weak just before and just after the turn, the actual error that may arise is likely to be very small.

Rigid navigational rules are likely to make tidal-stream application unnecessarily difficult. Up-dating the EP every exact hour during a passage is inconvenient if the time of HW at the standard port also occurs at or about each exact hour. The task is simplified by plotting the EP at half-past each hour so that only a single tidal vector is used. The next HW is likely to occur at half-past each hour and an up-date of the EP for a half-hour period can be made before continuing to plot at the next set of convenient hourly intervals.

6 Passage Planning

The Need for Pre-Planning
The navigator has a wealth of information at his disposal, in charts, sailing directions, tide tables and tidal stream atlases. The object of passage planning is to organise this information into a logical sequence so that it is immediately accessible when required at sea.

The Overall Plan for a Cruise
There are a number of possible starting points for the yacht navigator planning a trip to sea. Unlike the large-ship navigator, he does not have a destination which he must reach to deliver a cargo or passengers and his destination is only likely to be fixed by circumstances outside his control if he is racing. He is much more likely to be limited by the time available to go sailing than by any other factor, so the first stage of navigational planning is a matter of deciding the general area in which to cruise. There are almost no rules for this initial phase, any decisions being dictated by the personal preferences and whims of the skipper and his crew. The only pitfall to avoid is being over ambitious, trying to fit too long a cruise into too short a time. It is unusual for a sailing boat of 8m (26ft) LOA to average more than 4 knots during a cruise, and most crews like to spend at least as much time in harbour as at sea, so it would probably be a mistake to plan on covering any more than 300 miles in a week.

For the purposes of this chapter it is assumed that decisions on cruising areas have already been made and the objective is to plan the passages between ports.

Charts
Chart-work has already been described in detail in Chapter 1, but there are a number of points concerning charts which relate particularly to passage planning.

A list of Admiralty charts, with plans showing their coverage, is given in the *Admiralty Chart Catalogue*. There is an abridged edition of the catalogue which covers north-west European sea areas. Catalogues and the charts themselves are available from chart agents. The larger chart agents will also be able to provide foreign charts, or advise on how best to obtain them.

The Chart Outfit

Ideally, every available chart of the cruising area should be on board, but this ideal is likely to be thwarted by the high cost of a complete chart outfit. It is a sound maxim that the largest scale chart available should always be used for navigation, but one of the skills peculiar to the yachtsman is to decide which charts he may do without. There are no hard and fast rules upon which to base this decision, but there are some general guidelines.

A small scale chart of the whole cruising area is invaluable for general reference and planning. In any area where it is intended to spend some time exploring the coast, the largest scale charts are essential. In other areas through which passages are to be made, it is not unreasonable to carry only the coastal passage charts and not the large-scale harbour and harbour approach charts. In the event of having to use a harbour unexpectedly, a Pilot book may provide sufficient information to navigate the main channel in reasonable safety.

Foreign Charts

For cruising on foreign coasts more detailed charts are often available from the country which is being visited. There is some international standardisation of chart styles and symbols, but different countries still maintain a degree of national identity. Norwegian charts, for instance, use symbols which are smaller than those on Admiralty charts. Thus, they are able to include more detail in the narrow fiords which characterise the west coast, but an Englishman using their charts has to learn a slightly different set of conventional symbols and become familiar with a different style of presentation. Other countries also produce charts designed to meet the special needs of the small craft navigator. The Dutch Hydrographic Department, for instance, publishes a special series of plans, in A2 book form, for their inland waterways. The complete series is reissued every year so that it is kept up to date with the often dramatic changes which occur as the result of land-reclamation programmes. Foreign charts cannot readily be bought in the UK, although, given plenty of time, most chart agents can obtain them. In many foreign countries charts are sold by bookshops in seaside towns and it may be easier to delay buying foreign charts until arrival in the country concerned. As well as being easier to obtain, the charts are likely to be more up to date.

Chart Corrections

One task which needs to be undertaken before starting to use charts for passage planning, or for any other purpose, is to correct them up to date. Corrections are promulgated by the Hydrographic Department in *Weekly Editions of Notices to Mariners*, and any chart agent will post them regularly for a handling charge and the cost of post and packing. Alternatively, they can be collected, free of charge, from Admiralty chart agents or Mercantile Marine Offices.

Chart corrections should be inserted in waterproof ink (a very sharp pencil is an alternative for those who dislike working with waterproof ink), and the year and number of each correction should be noted in the bottom left-hand corner of the chart. Each notice shows the number of the last correction to the charts affected, so it is possible to check that no correction has been missed. One of the drawbacks of using foreign charts is that corrections to them are much more difficult to obtain.

In addition to the chart corrections published in the main body of *Notices to Mariners* each edition also contains reprints of radio navigational warnings issued during the week. These usually refer to temporary changes to charted features and there is a numbered series of warning messages for each area of the world. Those which are of most interest to British yachtsmen are the NAVAREA 1 series ('Navigational Warnings for the North East Atlantic'). Each week a summary of mobile drilling rigs and oil-exploration platforms is included in the NAVAREA 1 series. These large, well-lit structures can be extremely useful aids to navigation if their positions are kept charted up to date.

A special category of notices, Temporary (T) and Preliminary (P) notices, merits particular attention. As their name suggests, these notices are of a transient nature and they are therefore not inserted on charts by chart agents. Some T and P notices remain in existence for years, so it is a good idea to check that none apply to a new chart when it is first used.

A list of T and P notices in force is published each year in the annual summary of *Notices to Mariners*. Another section of *Notices to Mariners* lists new editions of charts. A new edition is much more than just a reprint; it is issued because there are such major changes to the area that it would be impractical to notify them by the normal small correction procedure.

The *Admiralty Lists of Lights* and *Lists of Radio Signals* are also kept up to date by corrections promulgated in *Notices to Mariners*. Because of their bulk and cost these books are seldom carried on board yachts, but it is worth glancing through the list of corrections to ensure that there are no important alterations — for instance, to radio beacons — which should be noted in the current edition of the nautical almanac. The almanacs go to press in the summer of the previous year, so they need to be brought up to date before the start of the sailing season.

Notices to Mariners: Small craft Edition

A special small craft edition of *Notices to Mariners* is published quarterly. This edition includes corrections to charts which are of concern only to craft drawing 2·5m (8ft) or less, and its geographical limits are the British Isles and near European continent. It may be purchased from chart agents.

Although the small craft edition of *Notices to Mariners* does not provide such up-to-date corrections to charts, it is considerably easier to use than the full weekly editions and for the yachtsman with a relatively small number of charts, most of which are unlikely to be affected by any one weekly edition of *Notices to Mariners*, the small craft editions are an extremely convenient source of correctional information.

Sailing Directions

Three types of sailing directions are available: the *Admiralty Sailing Directions (Pilots)*, yachtsmen's sailing directions, and cruising guide books. The Admiralty Pilots are intended to supplement the information shown on charts, covering all navigable waters which might be used by craft drawing over 1m (3ft). However, they are written primarily for the big ship navigator and are only of limited use to the yachtsman. They are, however, the authoritative reference book for harbour-entry signals.

Yachtsmen's Sailing Directions

Yachtsmen's sailing directions are published by cruising clubs and associations and by commercial publishing companies. They give explicit directions for harbour approaches and pilotage, frequently supported by sketch plans and photographs. Ideally, they should be used in conjunction with large-scale charts, although for many harbours it is perfectly possible to enter and leave using only the sketch plan and notes in the sailing directions and, in the case of very small harbours and remote anchorages, the sailing directions are the only information available.

Sailing directions generally include information on the shore facilities available in any harbour, such as the yacht clubs, boat-yards, marine engineers, fuel, water and stores.

Cruising Guides

There is no precise dividing line between sailing directions and cruising guides, but in general a cruising guide gives little precise pilotage information and is more concerned with general descriptions of harbours and anchorages which may be visited by yachts. The cruising guide is therefore useful in deciding whether or not a harbour or general area is worth visiting, but is of limited use for strictly navigational purposes.

Correcting Sailing Directions

Admiralty Sailing Directions are kept up to date by the periodic issue of supplements. Some yachtsmen's sailing directions are supported by a similar type of correctional service, but the resources available to a publisher or cruising club are limited in comparison with those of the Hydrographic Department, so the correctional service is generally much less comprehensive than for the official publications. When yachtsmen's sailing directions are being used it must be remembered that they may be out of date. In unstable areas where sand bars and banks are liable to change, yachtsmen's sailing directions which have been in print for a number of years should be used with caution and details of characteristics of lights and other navigational aids should be checked with official publications or up-to-date charts whenever possible.

A list of yachtsmen's sailing directions and cruising guides which are currently available is obtainable from the RYA.

A Passage-planning Check List

Having decided upon a cruising area and obtained the necessary charts and sailing directions, the detail of passage planning can begin. The variables which will affect the plan are: the earliest date at which it will be possible to sail; the lastest date by which the passage must be completed; the likely passage speed to the boat; the dangers to be avoided; and the tidal heights, tidal-stream rates and directions for the days in question. The actual and forecast weather are also likely to have a considerable bearing, but as the planning may be done days or even weeks in advance the weather is likely to be a factor which modifies, or even cancels, the plan at the last moment.

Fig 6.1 (overleaf) shows a check list which puts these variables into a convenient order for consideration and lists the points which should emerge in the planning process. It is particularly suitable for passages of up to about 100 miles.

Non-navigational Considerations

The check list assumes that the navigator has already decided his destination and the earliest time at which he will be able to sail — in other words, that he already has a general idea of the overall plan for his cruise. The list is concerned only with the navigational aspects of the plan and the skipper may consider that non-navigational aspects are of overriding importance. For instance, it may be navigationally convenient to sail at 0400, but with a crew who are not used to the boat or who have not been to sea for a while, going to sea before breakfast is likely to be a disaster and sailing must be delayed at least until 0900, or even until the corresponding afternoon tide.

Preparing Charts and Publications

Sections 2 and 3 of the check list are concerned with charts and publications, which have been discussed earlier in this chapter. If a number of charts are involved in a passage, it is worth arranging them in the order in which they are going to be used and inserting a passage serial number on each chart, in pencil, above the label on the back so that the next chart can be found quickly even if they have been jumbled in the wrong order when stowed.

129

1. FROM:	TO:	Distance:	n.m.
at (approx)*	at (approx)*		

* Consider probable route from small scale chart

2. CHARTS REQUIRED FOR PASSAGE:

corrected to A.N.M. edition:

3. TIMES OF H.W. AT REFERENCE PORT FOR TIDAL STREAM ATLAS

Port: Date/Times:

Port: Date/Times:

Tidal streams critical at: Times favourable

* Consider suitable sailing time in Section 1   Days from springs:

4. NOTES IN SAILING DIRECTIONS

ENTER NAME OF BOOK AT TOP OF COLUMN AND APPROPRIATE PAGE NUMBERS FOR EACH SECTION

Book:		
Dangers:		
Local Regs:		
Tidal Streams:		
Marks:		
Directions:		

5. TIDAL CURVES

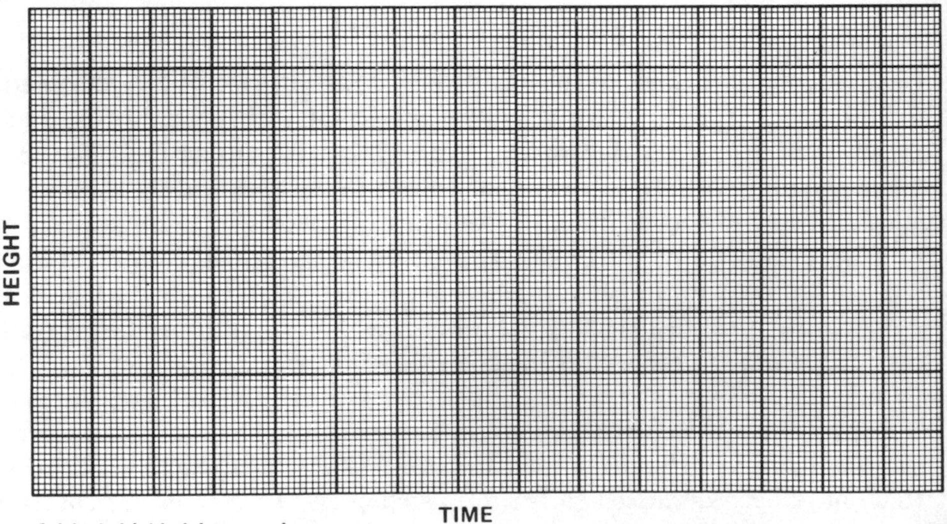

HEIGHT

TIME

Critical tidal heights over bars:-

* Now fill in approximate times in Section 1   Decide probable route from large and small scale charts

Fig 6.1 Passage planning check list

130

6. OPEN SEA PASSAGES

From	To	Courses to make good	Approx. distance	Remarks

7. HARBOURS OF REFUGE AVAILABLE IN CASE OF ADVERSE WEATHER

Port	Access Easy/Difficult	Tidal Considerations	Degree of shelter

8. DANGERS EN ROUTE

Danger	Marked by	Clearing lines

9. VISUAL AIDS AND RADIO BEACONS AVAILABLE

REEDS/A.L.R.S. Vol II Pages:-

10. BBC SHIPPING FORECAST RECEIVED AND NOTED AT:

Local Weather Report received at:

Actual Weather before sailing at: Wind: Weather:

Visibility: Baro: Sea: Swell:

Forecast that might render departure from plan necessary has been considered?

* REVIEW TIMES IN SECTION 1

It is possible to spend hours reading the sailing directions relevant to a passage. For quick reference at sea a note of important page numbers, or a system of markers in the book is useful. Loose slips of paper inserted between pages are often used for this purpose in big ships, but in yachts they tend to be impractical as sailing directions are often used in an open cockpit, where the markers blow away as soon as the book is opened.

Tidal Considerations

Both tidal heights and tidal-stream directions tend to form 'gates' to the yacht on passage. A bar at a harbour entrance is clearly an impassable barrier when the depth of water over it is less than the draught (plus a reasonable safety margin) and a contrary tidal stream of anything over 3 knots is likely to reduce a sailing boat's speed over the ground to such an extent that it is hardly worth fighting it.

Tidal Streams

The simplest method of examining tidal streams is to insert the dates and times to which it applies on each page of the tidal stream atlas. The relevant information can then be extracted quickly and easily for passage planning and during the passage itself. Tidal stream atlases do not entirely tell the full story on predicted rates. The tidal diamonds on large-scale charts often give a more accurate indication in harbour entrances. Sailing directions mention eddies and counter-currents which cannot be shown in the atlases because their extent is so small that the scale of the chartlets precludes the inclusion of such detail.

As a general rule, planning for tidal streams is a matter of adjusting sailing times to take advantage of the best favourable flow and avoid adverse flow. One addition to this overall concept is that in areas of very fast streams where overfalls are known to exist it is sometimes necessary to plan to transit a particular area at the time of slack water or to avoid it altogether.

Tidal Heights

Tidal heights are most easily displayed for planning purposes by drawing the appropriate curves, using the method described on page 120. Once this has been done, it is relatively easy to see the times between which it will be possible to cross a bar or bank. The safety margin which must be allowed depends on a number of factors. In general, the tide will not vary from its predicted height because of unusual barometric pressure or wind direction by more than one metre, so in calm conditions this is a reasonable margin to allow. In rough water, however, the danger of crossing a shallow bar arises from breaking seas rather than the risk of grounding. With onshore winds and a strong ebb stream, many bars give rise to dangerous sea conditions but with a flood stream they are safe. In strong onshore winds it may be necessary to accept a contrary flood stream for leaving harbour in order to find relatively flat sea conditions over the bar.

Planning adequate height of tide to give clearance over shoals and arranging favourable streams at the beginning of a passage is simply a matter of adjusting the time of sailing. At the end of a passage it is more difficult because passage speed under sail is an unknown quantity. On relatively short passages it may be possible to keep the speed up to the required average by the strategic use of the engine or to slow down to a more comfortable and manageable speed by reducing sail. The required passage speed may have to be considered in relation to streams and tidal heights throughout the planning of the passage and may be of vital importance in cruising areas such as the Channel Islands where the tidal range and the rates of streams are unusually large.

Daylight and Darkness

For some passages and unlit harbour entrances daylight is essential. As a general rule, it is easier to make a landfall at night, as the characteristics of navigational lights are easier to identify than the shape of an unfamiliar coastline. It is also desirable to time the first entry into an unfamiliar harbour so that the Sun is astern and certainly to avoid having to identify new marks against a low Sun.

During a cruise, one is usually aware of the time of evening twilight, as it changes very little each day and most people have a general awareness of the time of last light in the evening. First light in the morning, however, is long before most people are awake, so it may be necessary to refer to an almanac to find out the time it occurs.

Both the *Admiralty Nautical Almanac* and yachtsmen's nautical almanacs list times of morning and evening twilight. The Admiralty almanac lists both civil and nautical twilight and *Reed's* lists only civil twilight. At civil twilight the Sun is 6° below the horizon and at nautical 12°. At civil twilight the brighter planets are clearly visible to the naked eye and the brightest navigational stars are just discernible through a sextant telescope; the horizon is still clearly visible. At nautical twilight it is difficult to see the horizon unless there is a Moon or a background of artificial light.

The times of twilight listed in the almanac apply to the Greenwich meridian. East of Greenwich, twilight occurs 4 minutes earlier for each degree of E longitude and to the west 4 minutes later for each degree of W longitude.

Almanacs also list times of Moonrise and set and the phases of the Moon. A high full Moon will frequently give enough light to navigate a channel which would be impossible in total darkness.

Selection of Tracks

Deciding the detail of the route is a matter of remembering the simple fact that the shortest distance between two points is a straight line. The straight line will have to be amended to give navigational hazards adequate clearance, make the best possible use of tidal streams, take account of shipping lanes, and in some cases avoid the danger of a lee shore and take advantage of weather shores.

Distance off Dangers

There can be no hard and fast rules for the distance off dangers to plan. In calm weather, with a large-scale chart and a steep-to coast, it may be perfectly safe to round a headland a boat's length to seaward. This distance will have to be increased in onshore winds and if only a small-scale chart is available, to up to 2 miles from the furthest seaward off-lying danger, possibly many miles from the land itself. Similarly, a shoal which is well buoyed may be skirted closely but an unmarked shoal, passed several hours after the last reliable fix was obtained, should be given a berth of at least a mile plus about 10 per cent of the distance run since the last reliable fix.

On a coastal passage it can be dangerous to give a danger too wide a berth, if by doing so the yacht is unnecessarily taken so far from the land that it is impossible to identify marks for visual fixing. One danger may be avoided by giving it a wide berth, but the next may not, because of uncertainty as to the yacht's position.

Other Shipping

Busy shipping lanes are as much a hazard as rocks and shoals to a small boat. Apart from the danger of being run down, the presence of a large number of .ships is bound to distract the skipper's attention from the business of sailing and navigation. There are also specific rules in the *International Regulations for Preventing Collisions at Sea* which govern the conduct of small craft in narrow channels and in separation lanes.

If a big-ship buoyed channel must be used or crossed there are two simple rules: if following the direction of the channel, keep to the starboard side; and if crossing it, do so at right angles. In many instances, it is possible for yachts to navigate outside buoyed channels and in busy areas it is sensible to plan to follow tracks on the shallow-water side of the buoys.

In areas of high traffic density, one-way systems of traffic lanes, with separation zones between them, have been established. Fig 6.2 shows the separation scheme in the Dover Straits. The rules for these are that all craft should follow the general direction of traffic flow, small craft should avoid impeding the general flow of traffic and, if obliged to cross a separation scheme, should do so as nearly as practicable at right angles. To comply with the spirit of these rules, in a yacht speed should not be allowed to fall below

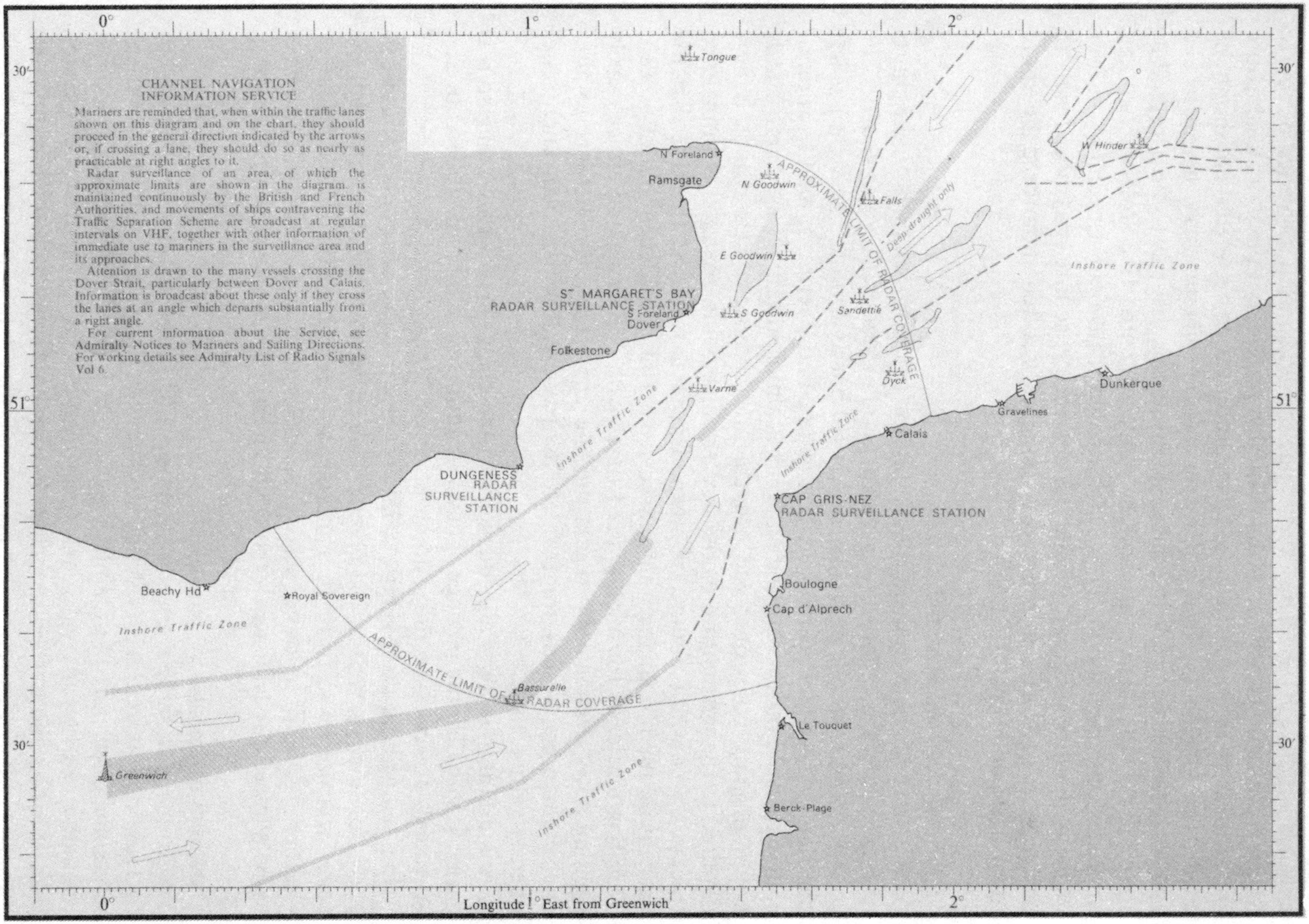
CHANNEL NAVIGATION INFORMATION SERVICE
Mariners are reminded that, when within the traffic lanes shown on this diagram and on the chart, they should proceed in the general direction indicated by the arrows or, if crossing a lane, they should do so as nearly as practicable at right angles to it.
Radar surveillance of an area, of which the approximate limits are shown in the diagram, is maintained continuously by the British and French Authorities, and movements of ships contravening the Traffic Separation Scheme are broadcast at regular intervals on VHF, together with other information of immediate use to mariners in the surveillance area and its approaches.
Attention is drawn to the many vessels crossing the Dover Strait, particularly between Dover and Calais. Information is broadcast about these only if they cross the lanes at an angle which departs substantially from a right angle.
For current information about the Service, see Admiralty Notices to Mariners and Sailing Directions. For working details see Admiralty List of Radio Signals Vol 6.
0°
1°
2°
30′
51°
30′
Tongue
N Foreland
Ramsgate
N Goodwin
E Goodwin
S Goodwin
Sᵀ MARGARET'S BAY RADAR SURVEILLANCE STATION
S Foreland
Dover
Folkestone
Varne
DUNGENESS RADAR SURVEILLANCE STATION
Beachy Hd
Royal Sovereign
Inshore Traffic Zone
APPROXIMATE LIMIT OF RADAR COVERAGE
Bassurelle
Greenwich
Falls
Deep draught only
Sandettié
Dyck
W Hinder
Dunkerque
Gravelines
Calais
CAP GRIS-NEZ RADAR SURVEILLANCE STATION
Boulogne
Cap d'Alprech
Le Touquet
Berck-Plage
Longitude 1° East from Greenwich

Fig 6.2 The traffic separation scheme in the Dover Strait

about 3 knots in light winds before the engine is started; if the wind is dead ahead when crossing the lanes, the engine should be used, provided of course that it is powerful enough to give reasonable progress; if possible, the inshore zones rather than the traffic lanes or separation zone between them should be used. The presence of a traffic separation scheme may necessitate a considerable detour from the direct line, but this just has to be accepted as ships using the lanes are often navigating to fine tolerances, and unpredictable behaviour by a yacht could cause an extremely serious incident. Failure to comply with the correct procedure may also result in prosecution as traffic in separation schemes is often monitored by shore radar and patrol craft.

Significance of the Planned Track

At this stage of the plan there is a temptation to draw firm lines on the charts and label them as 'courses to make good'. Moderation is needed. The courses to make good, or tracks, are useful but as soon as the yacht has left her planned track, because of adverse winds, bad steering or an alteration of course to avoid other craft, the old track is almost meaningless. There is little point in going back onto the original line because a new course is now required to the destination or the next turning point. Fixation with planned tracks is a common failure of inexperienced navigators, the fact that the yacht is on the line giving a misplaced feeling of confidence that all is well. This fixation leads to much wasted time, with the navigator unnecessarily fighting adverse streams to regain the line and having a reluctance to alter course for other vessels for fear of failure to follow the plan and conse-quently getting lost.

It is useful to draw planned tracks on the charts because by doing so it is easier to visualise the passage. They will almost certainly be rubbed out and amended, however, so they should be drawn lightly.

In a sailing boat there is little point in trying to work out courses to steer to allow for tidal streams at the planning stage because the speed through the water will not be known. In a motor yacht it is possible, although heavy weather may result in lower speeds than anticipated and leeway will also have to be allowed for later when the wind direction and strength are known.

Harbours of Refuge

Traditionally, a sailing vessel putting to sea is sailing *towards* as opposed to *to* a destination. It is accepted that stress of weather may result in her putting into some other port. At the planning stage it is worth taking a close look at the harbours of refuge which may be available. This is a matter of examining ease of access and degree of shelter. For harbours at which tidal height is an important consideration, it is worth sketching the tidal curve for the period during which it might be used.

Under this general heading it is also a good idea to check the chart coverage to make sure that if, for any reason, it is necessary to go past the destination the yacht is not going to sail off the edge of the available charts.

Time spent reading sailing directions and studying charts for harbours of refuge will not be repaid on every passage, but it will never be time wasted. If it is necessary to use one of these harbours it will be because of severe weather, gear failure, illness or injury. Under such circumstances a pre-prepared harbour entry plan will be well worth all the time spent preparing it and the other plans which have never been used.

Navigational Hazards

Having completed the bulk of the detailed planning work, it is worth having an overall look at the route in order to identify the navigational hazards which may have to be avoided. Some dangers do not stand out particularly prominently on the charts and it is useful to highlight them by a heavy pencil line showing the limits of navigable water. The plan should have allowed an adequate clearance for all dangers but the planned tracks may not be followed. Where it is possible to use a clearing bearing to give positive avoidance of a danger the appropriate bearing should be noted on the chart, or if no prominent object is suitably placed a note of the minimum safe sounding may be used.

Visual and Radio Aids

Some thought needs to be given to the actual means by which the yacht will be navigated during the passage. It is useful to indicate, by means of range circles, the distances off lights at which they should be sighted in clear weather.

Similar circles showing the effective ranges of radio beacons are also useful and these should be annotated to show the frequency, call-sign and sequence number of the beacon. This can save a considerable amount of time and effort looking up radio information during the passage.

If a number of passages are likely to be made across the same stretch of open water it is useful to construct a bearing lattice on the passage chart from the beacons which will be used. Fig 4.6 (p85) shows a lattice for the Solent to Cherbourg area. With this type of lattice, bearings can be plotted quickly and easily with the chart folded and the method is therefore particularly useful in small boats which do not have chart tables on which an unfolded chart can be spread. In practice, it is easier to use different colours rather than different styles of line for each beacon.

Planning Anchorages

The detailed planning of harbour entries and departures is an integral part of passage planning, but as the technique has already been described in Chapter

5 it is not intended to elaborate on it here. One special case of pilotage planning, however, is the planning of an anchorage. The factors which have to be taken into account include:

> Shelter, from present and forecast wind, sea and swell.
> Clear of fast tidal streams.
> Depth of water, deep enough to float throughout swinging circle at low water, shallow enough at high water for the cable available.
> Clear of fairways, shipping lanes and ferry routes.
> Holding ground.
> Proximity to landing place.
> Clear of other moored and anchored craft.
> Clear exit if necessary to leave at short notice or in darkness.
> Adequate marks to find selected spot.

Most of these are self-explanatory and need no elaboration. They will not all apply in every case, but most of them need to be considered when looking for an anchor berth.

The most difficult forecast to make about open or semi-sheltered anchorages is whether or not they will be clear of swell. General rules are that a ground swell will always be felt in the lee of small islands and close to areas of fast tidal streams and that a swell will refract around headlands up to an angle of about 90°.

The size of swinging circle needed will depend upon the depth of water. As a general guide, the minimum amount of chain cable to use is three times the depth at high water and double this amount is needed for security in strong winds or fast tidal streams. Using warp instead of chain, five times the depth at high water is the absolute minimum for reasonable holding. For planning purposes, it is reasonable to ignore the catenary of the cable and assume that the radius of the swinging circle will be the amount of cable veered plus the length of the boat.

Clay, mud and sand, in that order, provide the best holding ground. Gravel and shingle are poor, but usable, and no anchor is likely to be much use on a rocky bottom as it will either drag or become permanently fast in a fissure in the rock. (The possible exception is a very heavy fisherman which may hold in light winds and slack water simply by virtue of its weight.) Thick weed, such as is found in parts of the west coast of Scotland and the Channel Islands, may prevent the anchor from reaching the seabed. The anchor will then slide over the weed, collecting a bundle of fronds around the flukes. Anchoring in this type of area is possible only if the anchor is heavy enough to penetrate the weed to hold in the ground beneath.

Flexibility of Planning
The planning check list on which this chapter is based has been used extensively during Yachtmaster practical courses and it has been found

generally satisfactory. Its use is advocated for anyone who has limited experience of navigation in order to prevent any oversight of important aspects and to introduce some logic into a process in which many factors have to be considered and in which different factors will be of paramount importance in differing circumstances. Thorough planning of a passage can take as long as the passage itself takes to sail, but experience in any area will considerably reduce the planning time as the navigator becomes familiar with the harbours, features and tidal patterns.

There is always a temptation to be over-elaborate in planning passages in unfamiliar waters, to write copious notes, cover the chart with lines and fill notebooks with jottings. The temptation must be resisted. Notebooks can be useful if the information recorded in them is brief enough for easy reference. Only the most important lines and markings should appear on the chart, otherwise they will be lost among the irrelevancies.

Before putting to sea, someone ashore should have an outline of the intended route and destination. If the yacht is long overdue at her destination, it will then be relatively simple for the Coastguard to initiate a search for her in the right general area, particularly if they already have details of the boat on a Small Boat Safety Scheme card. Any arrangements made before going to sea for someone ashore to alert the rescue services should stress, however, that light winds may prolong a passage or heavy weather may cause the yacht to seek shelter, possibly in an anchorage from which telephone communication is not available. A VHF radio-telephone makes it easy to allay anxiety (see RYA booklet G22).

Finally, the plan must never be allowed to assume more importance than it deserves. It should be drawn up with as much care as possible, but it must be reviewed at the time of the latest weather forecast prior to sailing and in the light of subsequent weather conditions and forecasts. It contains navigational information which was used on the basis of other factors prevailing at the time and changes in non-navigational factors, such as the strength of the crew or the material condition of the yacht, may be of much greater significance than purely navigational matters and dictate a change of plan.

7 Passage Making

A Self-checking System of Navigation

An analysis of incidents in which groundings of ships have occurred reveals a common trend running through all of them. At the time of the grounding, or at least a very short time before the grounding, those responsible for the navigation of the ship believed that they knew her position and that she was on a safe course. Only in a tiny minority of cases was there doubt in her navigator's mind as to the ship's actual position. Setting aside the very small number of incidents in which ships grounded on uncharted hazards, it is also possible to identify at least six distinct navigational errors, or short cuts from standard navigational practice, which contributed to each grounding, and without which the grounding would probably not have occurred.

Very few grounding incidents leading to loss of life or damage to property occur because a yacht is 'lost'. They are more often the result of the yacht being 'misplaced'. The navigator thinks he knows his position and runs aground because of a false assumption, a misinterpretation rather than a lack of navigational information. The first requirement for any system of navigation, therefore, is that it should be self-checking and the mental approach of the navigator should be of open-mindedness. There is always a temptation to try to make navigational information fit in with the navigator's general feeling of where he is or where he wants to be. This is a dangerous attitude.

A safe attitude involves a completely unprejudiced approach to all positional information, allowing comparison of independent methods. There are nearly always two independent methods available to find a yacht's position at sea: by estimated position from course steered, distance run, leeway, tidal set and drift, and by fixing, from either visual or radio bearings. A check of the depth by echo-sounder can also confirm that the plotted position is not grossly in error, as can a general look round to see that any land or navigational marks appear to be in the expected position or are presenting the expected aspect.

Safe navigation might be considered as a negative process because it involves discarding bad information and gross errors rather than achieving pin-point accuracy. This is the art as opposed to the science of navigation, the continuous assessment of the relative merits of the presently available sources of positional information. It calls for a rare ability to admit to mistakes and, if there is marked and apparently inexplicable disagreement between positions achieved from different sources, the courage to admit that something has gone badly wrong and heave to, or even reverse course until the difference has been reconciled.

The navigation of a yacht is seldom a one-man job and it is safer to involve several people because they are likely to spot each other's mistakes. On a passage of any length it is convenient for one of the watch on deck to do the routine navigation during his watch. It is possible that a mistake he makes will not be discovered until some time after the next watch has taken over and he will then have to check back through his work. This sort of co-operation is only possible if everyone uses the same system of conventional plotting symbols and works reasonably neatly and logically.

Navigational Records

An accurate record of navigational information is essential to allow chart-work to be checked whenever the need arises. Notes and scribbled calculations in the margin of the chart quickly become an illogical muddle and loose sheets of paper tend to get lost. The right place for navigational information is a notebook or log-book.

There are a number of forms of yacht log-book available with ruled columns and boxes for recording information. In general, these tend to make provision for too much information and a very rigid form of log-book is tedious to complete and wasteful of space. During a passage there are certain standard and repetitive items that need to be recorded. Fig 7.1 shows a convenient layout of log-book for passage making: columns 1—4 give all the information needed to work up the estimated position and columns 5 and 6 provide a continuous record of the two most important aspects of the weather.

TIME	LOG	COMPASS COURSE STEERED	ESTIMATED LEEWAY	WIND DIR/STR	BARO-METER	REMARKS
1025	—	—	—	SW/3	1012	Slipped mooring, under engine.
1058	121·4	—	—	—	—	Fairway buoy ⊥ . Set full main + No 2 genoa, engine off. Set course 180° (C)
1135	123·7	182°(C)	5°	SW/5		Wind increasing. 1 slab in main.
1200	126·1	175° (C)	7°	SW/5	1011	Departure fix on chart.
1300	131·4	178° (C)	7°	SW/5	1010·5	Vis 6 miles & reducing. Rain started.
1400	136·1	173° (C)	7°	SW/5-6	1010	

Fig 7.1 Suggested layout for a logbook

As an alternative to a column for barometric reading a more informative record can be compiled by plotting the reading on graph paper. This, in effect, produces a barograph trace and gives a more explicit picture of the barometric trend.

These columns can easily be ruled in a hard-backed exercise book. It will seldom be convenient to write up the log exactly at hourly intervals. Times of getting under way, passing significant buoys, taking departure fixes or making course alterations are all occasions which call for log entries and they will seldom coincide with whole hours, so it is sensible to leave the time column blank and fill in actual times as entries are made. During a passage of any length, hourly log entries, preferably at each whole hour, are useful. If only spasmodic entries are made it is extremely difficult for the helmsman to record the actual course steered. It is important that the log entry is a true record rather than a mere acknowledgement that the helmsman knows what course he was asked to steer. It is often much easier to steer a few degrees off the required course to gain a little extra speed, avoid the possibility of an accidental gybe, or simply because the boat seems to want to sail in that direction. As long as there is adequate sea room on a long passage a discrepancy between the required and actual course is unlikely to be of much importance, but the navigator must know what course has actually been steered, otherwise he will never be able to work out an accurate estimated position.

There is no advantage in recording the course steered as anything other than compass. The remarks column should include the sail carried, course alterations, times at which the engine is started and stopped, engine revolutions, times of raising and dipping of lights, and any other information which is of general or navigational interest.

It is probably better to keep a separate notebook for the actual details of fixes and for calculations which cannot be done without the use of pencil and paper. Recording fixes can be difficult in wet weather when a notebook taken into the cockpit is quickly transformed into pulp. One method of overcoming this problem is to develop the habit of writing the names of the lights or objects to be used in the notebook at the chart table, then going on deck to take the bearing, memorising only the last two digits of each and writing these into the notebook at the chart table and adding the first digits. Six digits are much easier to memorise than nine, and the chance of ambiguity as to the first digit of a bearing is negligible.

A well-kept log-book is much more than the means by which estimated positions are worked out. It is the information from which an accurate assessment of the yacht's and navigator's performance can be made. Over a period of time the log will show, perhaps, that landfalls at the end of reaching passages consistently turn out to be several miles to windward of the EP, from which it may be assumed either that leeway is being over-estimated or that the crew are unwittingly sailing to windward of the required course. At the end of a season it will be relatively easy to add up the total engine hours and decide whether a major overhaul is needed. A complete picture of the yacht's sailing characteristics will also have emerged — wind strengths in which various combinations of sail were carried and the progress made under them, and speed under power in the open sea — just the sort of information the skipper needs in order to make the right decisions during a cruise.

Coastal Navigation

During any apparently straightforward coastal passage there is a temptation simply to sail from one known mark to the next and not to navigate at all in the sense of using chart, compass, log and echo-sounder. This may be perfectly safe, but only if all the following questions can be answered in the affirmative:

1 Are good visibility and daylight guaranteed for the duration of the passage?
2 Am I sure that I know all the marks on this coast well enough for there to be no possibility of confusion?
3 Is there sufficient breadth of safe navigable water for an accurate knowledge of position at any time to be unimportant?
4 Do I know the tidal streams so well, or are they so weak, that I don't need to calculate allowance for them?

If the answer to any of the questions is no, there is a definite risk in not following a navigational routine designed to ensure positive safety.

On passage along an unfamiliar coast there is always a possibility of mis-identifying a fixing mark, assuming an erroneous position as a consequence and then running aground. Fig 7.2 (overleaf) shows the chart-work for a typical short coastal passage, from Torbay to Exmouth. The open-water distance from the Ore Stone to the mouth of the Exe is a little over 9 miles, and in good visibility Straight Point would be visible. For the purpose of this example, however, moderate visibility of 4–5 miles prevails.

Departure is taken from a fix half a mile to seaward of the Ore Stone at 0925 (Position A). Course is set, to counteract leeway and tidal stream, and with the present speed made good of 4 knots an estimated position is plotted ahead to 1000, position B. At 1000 a fix is taken and the log reading of 2·4 miles confirms that the speed made good has been maintained. The plotted fix, however, is some 3·5 cables from the EP. This is not an unreasonable discrepancy for the fix could well be in error by a cable or so, or the log could have under-read by this amount and the helmsman may well have steered a degree or two off the required course. The echo-sounder shows a depth of 21m which generally confirms that nothing is badly in error, although with the gently shelving sea bed off this part of the coast it would only indicate an exceptionally gross error in the position.

From the 1000 fix, a position is again estimated ahead, for half an hour

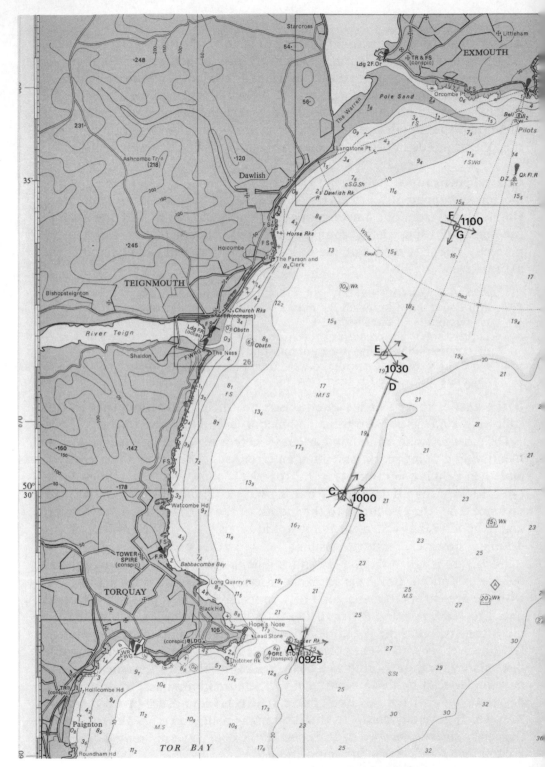

Fig 7.2 Chartwork for a short coastal passage

this time, to give position D. A fix at 1030 again gives a position ahead of the EP, confirming that the log is probably under-reading. The fix is not a particularly accurate one, which is not surprising as the three marks used are close to the limit of visibility and difficult to identify with certainty. The church on Dawlish sea-front, not shown as conspicuous, is a particularly vague mark, but by including it in the fix the navigator is trying to confirm that he has identified the correct building. In better visibility he might have used it as a fourth bearing simply to confirm that he really was looking at the right building, so that further up the coast, where suitable marks are few and far between, he has at least one positively identified reference point.

It is now apparent from the three fixes plotted that the yacht is making good a course some 5° to port of the one required, directly towards the seaward end of Pole Sand, so an alteration to starboard is made, and the EP plotted ahead to 1100, this time using the speed made good indicated by the fixes instead of by the log, to give position F. At 1050 Straight Point is sighted on the expected bearing and, 5 minutes later, the red and yellow DZ buoy. For the 1100 fix, at position G, there are only two suitable marks visible and they give a position (G) in close agreement with the 1100 EP. The navigator can now check that he is not being set towards the Pole Sand by watching the bearing of Straight Point Light, and at 1130 he should have the red and yellow DZ buoy abeam.

This was a very simple coastal passage which could, as it turned out, have been made simply by calculating the course to steer and setting out in the direction of Exmouth. An alteration of course of about 10° would have been needed when Straight Point was sighted and nothing appears to have been gained by working out three EPs and taking four fixes. But the story might have been very different. If visibility had deteriorated between 1030 and 1100, when fixing marks were difficult to see anyway, to about half a mile, the passage might well have ended on the Pole Sand; or if a light-meter had been stowed under the bridge deck, inducing a 25° deviation in the compass, the yacht might have headed out towards the Dorset coast in the vicinity of Bridport. Nothing would seem obviously wrong until Straight Point failed to appear. The disappearance of the land might be explained as a deterioration in visibility and the echo-sounder would give very little indication that all was not well. Situations such as these occur only on very rare occasions, but undoubtedly they do occur and it is only by a meticulous approach that the navigator can be certain that he will not be caught out by them.

Offshore Navigation

On an offshore passage the requirement for frequent fixes and comparisons with EPs are less important than when coasting, but the principle of running a self-checking system is exactly the same. The navigator must work in such a way that he avoids the possibility of gross error, but he has less information

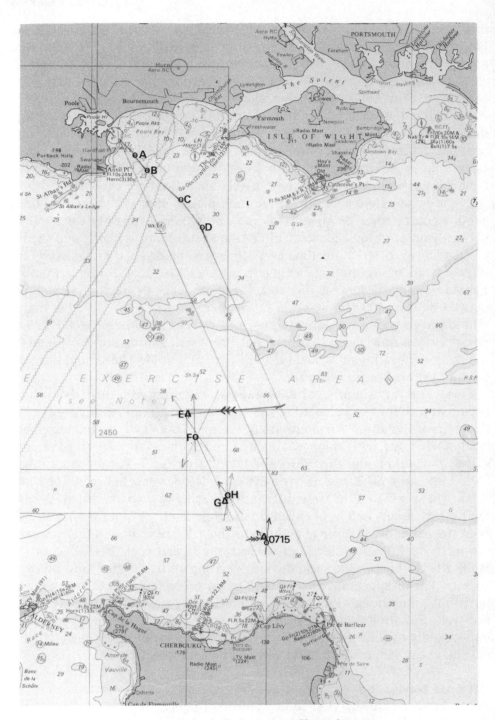

Fig 7.3 Chartwork for a cross-Channel passage

available to him as radio beacons some 30–50 miles distant cannot give him position lines with guaranteed accuracy of better than ± 5 miles.

To explain the general pattern of navigation it is convenient to take another example, this time the Channel crossing from Poole to Barfleur. The total distance between harbour entrances is some 65 miles, and with a passage speed of 4 knots the passage time will be just over 16 hours (Fig 7.3).

Departure is taken from Poole Fairway Buoy at 2000, half an hour before sunset and 3½ hours before HW Dover. In a sailing boat the navigator will not know his passage speed until he is at sea, although he may be able to make an earlier approximation from the forecast and the actual wind in the harbour.

The tidal streams (springs) likely to be encountered during the passage are:*

2000–2100	080°–2M
2100–2200	090°–1½M
2200–2300	090°–1M
2300–2359	255°– ¾M
0001–0100	265°–2½M
0100–0200	270°–2½M
0200–0300	270°–3M
0300–0400	260°–3M
0400–0500	255°–1½M
0500–0600	slack
0600–0700	080°–1½M
0700–0800	090°–3M
0800–0900	090°–3½M
0900–1000	100°–2M
1000–1100	100°–1M
1100–1200	310°–2M

After 1200 the streams around Pointe de Barfleur build up to a rate of 5 knots to the NW, so it is desirable to complete the passage by 1200. If it proves impossible to maintain the necessary speed, a decision will have to be taken either to divert to Cherbourg or to accept that between 1200 and about 1600 it will be almost impossible to round Pointe de Barfleur against the contrary stream.

Drawing out the tidal streams the resultant set over the full duration of the passage is just under 1 mile to the east, the equivalent of less than 0·1 knots, so it is hardly worth making any allowance for it. The yacht will, in fact, sail

*A slight oversimplification of the tidal streams is given, by simply taking the spring rates for successive hours from the tidal-stream atlas. In practice, this could not be done as successive high waters are not 12 hours apart, but the simplification makes the example easier to follow.

a course which passes first to the east of the direct line, back to cross it at about 0130, over to the west until about 0930, and then another short curve to the east. Her maximum distances off the direct line will be about 4½ miles to the east at 2300 and 8½ miles to the west at 0500. There is adequate safe water to follow this track so there is certainly nothing to be gained by trying to stay any closer to the rhumb line.

The early part of the trip is exactly like a coastal passage as far as the navigation is concerned. Fixes at 2030, 2100, 2200 and 2300 (positions A, B, C and D) confirm that the EP and fix positions are in agreement. No further visual fixes are possible, as the lights at Anvil Point, St Catherine's and The Needles are now out of range in the prevailing visibility. Of the available radio beacons only St Catherine's is close enough to give a bearing which is likely to be as accurate as the EP, so there is little point in doing more than taking a single round of beacons to confirm that the DF is working.

Navigation for the next few hours is a matter of up-dating the EP each hour from the course steered, log reading and estimates of tidal stream and leeway. This is a task which the watch on deck will probably do, possibly leaving the navigator free to take a few hours' sleep. His only worry at the moment is to maintain the 4 knots necessary to round Pointe de Barfleur before the start of the foul stream, and he may want to be woken if the speed drops to decide whether or not to start the engine. The 0015 shipping forecast will give an indication of the wind he can expect for the rest of the passage and if the speed does drop he will certainly have to take the forecast into account when deciding whether to start the engine and keep to the original plan, alter course and head for Cherbourg, or accept a longer passage to Barfleur.

Between 2300 and 0400 the distance run by log is 24·5 miles. This gives an EP at position E, 32 miles from Barfleur Harbour entrance. A radio fix is now certainly worth while, and position lines from Pointe de Barfleur, Fort de l'Ouest (Cherbourg) and St Catherine's indicate that the actual position is probably slightly to the east of the EP and 3 miles further on (position F).

The speed through the water is now 4·7 knots and the yacht has been sailing faster than originally expected so the course required must be reworked. At the present speed the ETA at Barfleur will be 1050, and the course to steer now differs substantially from the course to be made good.

Sunrise is at 0520 and the lights of the French coast are therefore unlikely to be in range before they are switched off. At 0600 a further radio fix (position H), this time using only the Fort de l'Ouest and Barfleur beacons, gives very close agreement with the EP (position G). At 0715 lighthouses on the coast are visible, and a fix at 0715 confirms that these are probably C Levi and Pointe de Barfleur. Navigation now continues as for a coastal passage, hopefully with increasing confidence as more marks on the shore and the off-lying beacons are identified.

148

On a Channel crossing like this one, it should be possible to maintain continuity in the navigation without ever having to start position finding without a datum from which to work. The initial departure phase of coastal navigation gives the EP against which the mid-channel radio fixes are checked, which in turn lead to EPs which provide a check against a gross error in the landfall fix.

The example above is illustrated on a single chart. In practice, it would be necessary to use several charts. Whenever the chart in use is changed the latest position should be transferred to the new chart by two independent means — for instance, by latitude and longitude and range and bearing from a conspicuous point which appears on both charts. This guards against the possibility of introducing a gross error during the change of charts.

When using a number of charts only one should be on the chart table at any time. If there are two charts of slightly different scale it is quite possible, particularly at night, for the latitude scale of the bottom chart to be left exposed and inadvertently used to measure a distance.

Landfalls

The landfall at the end of a Channel crossing or a longer offshore passage tends to be a time of apprehension for the navigator. In the passage just described, there was a relatively simple landfall because the navigator had kept his position up to date with radio fixes and EPs and there were two very conspicuous lighthouses available for a fix while still well offshore.

Under different circumstances, at the end of a prolonged heavy-weather passage, with no conveniently situated radio beacons, it can be extremely difficult to identify fixing marks with any certainty. High hills some distance inland often become visible when the coastline itself is still below the horizon and it is difficult to reconcile the navigator's view of the coast with the information shown on the chart. The photographs and sketches in the *Admiralty Sailing Directions* can help by showing the general shape of prominent features. If there are no off-lying dangers it may have to be accepted that a positive fix will not be possible for some time after the first sighting of land. At night the unambiguous characteristics of lighthouses solve this problem.

One aspect of the final approach to the coast which often causes unnecessary worry to inexperienced navigators is the difficulty of identifying the harbour entrance. There is understandable anxiety about finding the pier head or river entrance long before there is any real chance of identifying it. As long as reliable fixing is possible from other marks there is no danger in closing the coast to within a mile without identifying the actual destination, and this is frequently the only way to approach a harbour which does not itself have any conspicuous identifying features.

Navigational Strategy

Keeping track of position and sailing clear of dangers are not the navigator's only functions. He also has to decide the fastest course to the destination — although the fastest course will by no means always be the most direct. Frequently it will be quicker to stand inshore to keep out of a foul stream or offshore to make the best use of a favourable one; it may be faster to seek smoother water under a weather shore than to sail a direct course through a lumpy sea.

The ability to make decisions on the fastest route requires familiarity with the yacht's sailing characteristics and a detailed knowledge of the intricacies of tidal streams along any particular stretch of coast. Both can be acquired with certainty only by experience, although there are general rules which apply to all yachts and most coasts. Tidal streams are usually less strong close inshore and the stream usually turns inshore before it does offshore. The effect of waves on speed varies enormously from boat to boat — a shallow, beamy boat may be stopped almost dead by a short-head sea, whereas a deep boat with a fine entry may be affected relatively little by the same sea.

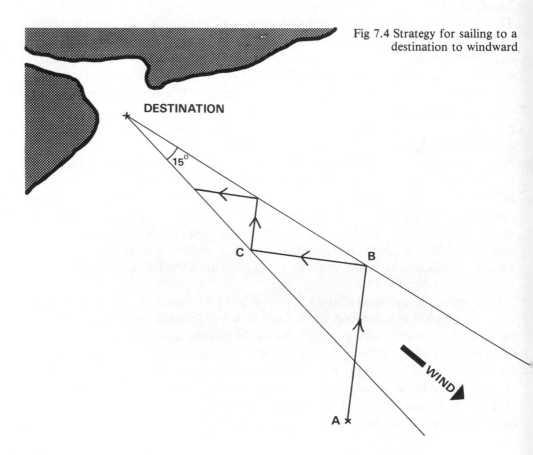

Fig 7.4 Strategy for sailing to a destination to windward

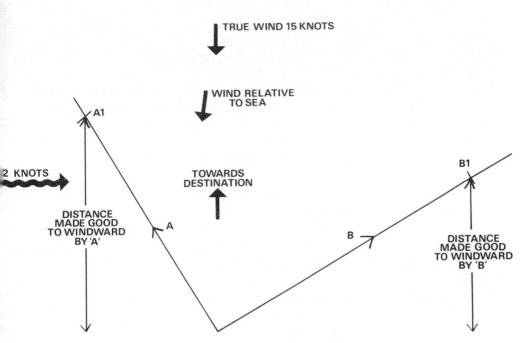

TRUE WIND 15 KNOTS

WIND RELATIVE
TO SEA

A1

2 KNOTS

TOWARDS
DESTINATION

B1

DISTANCE
MADE GOOD
TO WINDWARD
BY 'A'

A

B

DISTANCE
MADE GOOD
TO WINDWARD
BY 'B'

Fig 7.5 Advantage of a lee-bow tide

The sailing navigator frequently must decide on the most advantageous route to a windward destination. The general rule is to sail the most advantageous tack first, then make fairly short tacks to stay within 5–10° of the down-wind line from the objective (Fig 7.4). The reason for this course is that by staying directly down wind any change of wind direction will be advantageous. If the forecast predicts a change of wind direction there may be some advantage in planning the track to take advantage of the wind shift, but forecasters can seldom predict the time of a back or veer with sufficient certainty for the navigator to be able to bank on taking advantage of it. Large wind shifts frequently occur in summer during the morning when the sea breeze sets in and these are seldom mentioned in the shipping forecast because they occur only in a relatively small part of each sea area.

On a long cross-tide windward leg there is also some advantage to be gained by tacking to keep the stream on the lee-bow. A weather-going tide produces a relative freeing shift to the wind, a lee-going tide gives a heading shift (Fig 7.5).

It is impossible to be dogmatic about rules to apply when planning a route to windward because a number of factors may be involved and some of them are likely to depend on predictions which may be little better than intelligent guesses. The three variables which may have to be considered are tidal stream, degree of shelter and wind shifts. The only 'rule' is that the wind shifts are likely to be the most important consideration and also, unfortunately, the most difficult to predict.

Navigation at Anchor

It may seem paradoxical to suggest that navigation is necessary in an anchored yacht, but under certain conditions it is vital. As soon as the anchor is down bearings should be taken, if possible on objects which will be lit at night. It does not matter whether the objects used are charted — the aim is not to determine position but to be able to check that the anchor is holding. Ideally, transits are better than bearings because they can be checked more easily. As the stream changes the yacht will swing around her anchor so there will be some change in the anchor bearings, but, unless the objects used are very close or the transits very sensitive, the movement at the turn of the tide will be small.

Riding out a gale at anchor it may be necessary to keep one man permanently on watch to keep a continuous check on the anchor bearings. If the anchor does start to drag the first indication may well be the rumbling of the chain across the sea bed and this noise at any time other than the turn of the tide is a signal that the anchor bearings should be checked.

Navigation in Restricted Visibility

Fog is the navigator's worst enemy. It deprives him of the ability to see navigational marks and induces a sense of isolation from the rest of the world. The major hazard in fog is collision and a secondary hazard is grounding. To be sure of avoiding these the possibility of delay has to be accepted.

A number of precautions should be taken if the advent of fog seems imminent. Hoist the radar reflector (if it is not already secured aloft), make sure that the position on the chart is up to date and that the course does not pass dangerously close to navigational hazards which a reduction in visibility will make it impossible to avoid with certainty, and sail clear of shipping lanes.

Once visibility has closed in, the navigator's task is in many ways simpler than in clear weather. He is deprived of the ability to fix on marks at any distance, so he must make the best use he can of radio beacons, soundings and above all keep an accurate EP. All possible precautions must be taken to avoid risk of collision by avoiding shipping lanes and keeping the best possible look-out, by sight and sound. The importance of a really alert listening watch cannot be over emphasised. It is impossible to take an accurate bearing of a fog signal and its range is even more difficult to estimate, but the presence of a fog signal, whether it is from a ship or a navigational aid, is vital information.

The only insurmountable navigational problem which fog imposes is that it becomes impossible to navigate in areas where sight of shore marks is essential, thus making certain harbours and anchorages unapproachable.

In the open sea, out of sight of land, the state of visibility does not affect navigation. Close to the coast, if it seems likely that the fog will persist, an early decision whether or not it is navigationally safe to continue must be taken. If there is any doubt, the safe course of action is to sail into shallow water and anchor. The longer the fog lasts, the more imprecisely will the position be known, as the inevitable inaccuracies which exist in the data from which an EP is derived build up in proportion to the time elapsed since the last fix. Eventually, the inaccuracies become so large that there can be no guarantee of remaining clear of hazards and the yacht is forced out to sea, into the shipping lanes.

There are two navigational techniques which can be used in fog to continue a passage which would otherwise be impossible. These involve replanning the route so that frequent position checks are obtained from buoys or to conform to clearly defined depth-contour lines.

Buoy hopping involves planning tracks between buoys, preferably using buoys with fog signals, working out the course to steer between each as accurately as possible and keeping a good look-out and listening watch. In using this sort of navigation it is essential to keep a close watch on soundings to make sure that the yacht is not being set off track and to work out the log reading and time at which the next buoy should be reached. If the next buoy has not been sighted when the log reading shows that the distance has been run, it is extremely dangerous to start a search or sail on in the hope that the next mark will be sighted. Running for too long on EP is almost certain to result in becoming totally lost and eventually grounding or wandering into a shipping lane. It is much better to anchor while the position is still reasonably accurate and wait for an improvement in the visibility.

Fig 7.6 (overleaf) shows a typical situation in which depth-contour-lines can be used. At position A visibility closes in to a quarter of a mile and it would be unwise to continue directly towards the fairway buoy at the river entrance. EP navigation to within a quarter of a mile after a 15 mile run is not within the limits of guaranteed accuracy, even if the position at A is known accurately, which is itself unlikely. The best way to find the entrance would be to close the coast, until the 5m depth-contour-line is reached, then to continue in a series of zig-zags, standing out until the depth increases to 7m, then in again until it shoals to 5m and so on. Eventually, the starboard hand channel buoy should appear. This system of zigzags along a contour line is preferable to trying to steer along the contour, altering to port if the depth shoals, to starboard if it deepens. Trying to follow the contour line involves a number of random alterations of course, which are difficult to plot, whereas the deliberate zigzag with about 30° between legs is much easier to keep track of. Care must be taken to make the legs short enough to be certain that there is no possibility of sailing past the objective, and there must be an even slope to the sea bed with few irregular features for the method to be effective.

153

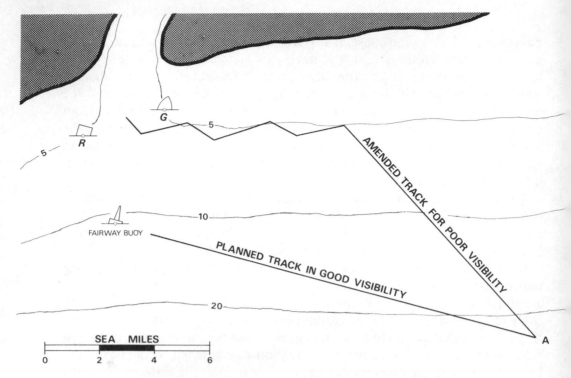

Fig 7.6 The use of a depth-contour line in restricted visibility

'Pool of Errors' Navigation

The navigator's aim should always be to keep an up-to-date position on the chart. Sometimes this is impossible to achieve, either because the EP is based on very out-of-date information, or more often because heavy weather makes it impossible to guarantee radio bearings, courses steered, leeway angles and log readings, with anything approaching accuracy. It may also be difficult to work at the chart table because the concentration needed to plot courses, distances and bearings in a gyrating boat requires an immunity to sea-sickness which few are lucky enough to have. A decision to give up any attempt at accurate navigation may have to be taken under extremely adverse conditions, the considerations to be taken into account being the actual danger of grounding or getting completely lost which have to be weighed against the drain on energy and stamina which will inevitably result from a ½-hour session at the chart table. In a small boat, where the skipper depends entirely on his own navigational ability, it may be more important to concentrate on the sailing and conserve energy than to be meticulous about navigation.

During a Channel crossing, it may be possible to say that at any time the yacht's position will be deducible from a known wake course, accurate to within ± 15°, a log reading accurate to within ±10 per cent of the distance run and a tidal-stream prediction accurate to within ±½ mile for every hour run.

154

Thus it may be possible to say that, for the next 12 hours, the yacht cannot possibly be in navigational danger, because even if the errors are the maximum in any direction there are no hazards she could hit. It would, in fact, be possible to draw an expanding figure on the chart, outside which the boat cannot possibly be, and inside which there are no hazards. This expanding figure is the 'pool of errors' and it will seldom be necessary to do more than roughly sketch it. The navigator will not know where he is within the 'pool of errors' but as long as he is not sharing it with a rock or shoal he knows that more accurate navigation need not be a high priority. In effect, he can guarantee safety by knowing where he is *not* rather than knowing exactly where he is.

The snag with this sort of navigation is that eventually a landfall has to be made and a harbour entrance located. If there is a conspicuous mark or light to give a safe lead into harbour and this can be located before the pool of errors impinges upon a hazard, the passage may be completed without recourse to more formal navigation. But if visibility is poor, there are unmarked off-lying dangers and an absence of convenient radio beacons, it may be necessary to heave-to offshore until the visibility improves or head for a harbour which is easier to approach than the original destination.

Pool-of-errors navigation is not recommended as standard practice. It is useful when the going is rough and the skipper is preoccupied with so many other tasks that he has no energy to spare for navigation. It is a definite risk, but it can be calculated, so it is certainly not an unjustifiable risk.

The Limits of Navigational Accuracy
Every navigator builds up an overall picture of his own limits of accuracy. The beginner tends to ask how accurate an instrument, say, a radio direction-finder, should be. There is never any definitive answer to this sort of question, other than the highly unsatisfactory, 'It all depends.' It depends upon a number of variables — in the hypothetical case of the radio direction-finder, the distance from the radio beacon, the sea state, the freedom from unknown deviation of the associated compass and, above all, the skill and experience of the operator.

It is important never to over-estimate the accuracy of navigation because, by doing so, it is possible to run into trouble simply by attempting to sail closer to danger than the system of navigation in use can guarantee safety. Table 7.1 (overleaf) gives an indication of the accuracy which should be achievable by an experienced yacht navigator. It must be stressed that this is not an objective list of accuracies of instruments and predictions which will be achieved by everyone. It is a subjectively compiled guide to the accuracy which a yacht navigator should be able to obtain within the limitations imposed by the current state of yacht navigational technology.

TABLE 7.1

SYSTEM	CALM CONDITIONS (Sea state 0-2)	MODERATE CONDITIONS (Sea state 3-5)	ROUGH CONDITIONS (Sea state 6+)	FACTORS AFFECTING ACCURACY
Shore transit	Exact	Exact	Exact	Clearly defined objects with long horizontal distance between
Compass bearing	±2°	±5°	±10°	Hand-bearing compass used clear of ferrous metal (not achievable with steel or composite hull)
Compass (Wake) course	±2°	±5°	±10°	Leeway may be difficult to determine in very rough weather
Distance by towed log	±50% Tends to under-read but distance small so error small	±5%	±5%	
Distance by hull-mounted log	±20%	±5%	±10%	
Radio bearing	±3°	±7°	±12°	Figures quoted for $\frac{2}{3}$ max range of beacon and strong audio signal. Shorter ranges may be more accurate, longer ranges less accurate; dependent also on sophistication of equipment
Depth by echo-sounder	All conditions ±5% of depth			Instruments must be adjusted or reading be corrected for depth of transducer
Distance by dipping distance of light	All condition ±5% of range			
Tidal stream predictions	All conditions ±10% of rate			Extreme and prolonged abnormal wind direction or barometric pressure may introduce large errors
Tidal height predictions	All conditions ±10% of range or ±1m, whichever is the greater			As tidal streams
Time	Should be measurable exactly in all conditions			

The inaccuracies which are inevitable because of the instruments and systems used are unlikely to give rise to difficulties or lead to danger. They should not be confused with gross errors, which arise from misuse and which are also almost inevitable, but which can be detected and eliminated by using a self-checking system of navigation.

The Authors

This book was written by an editorial team whose brief was to compile a manual of navigation based on the syllabus for the RYA/DoT Yachtmaster Offshore Certificate.

The members of the team were chosen for their knowledge of teaching or writing about navigation and their experience as yachtsmen:

BERNARD HAYMAN was for many years the editor of *Yachting World*, a magazine which is respected as the authoritative journal of international yachting. He has a long personal involvement in cruising, visiting most countries in Northern Europe and Scandinavia in his own yachts *Barbican* and *Barbican 2*.

MIKE LYNSKEY is a professional seaman, a lecturer in navigation in Liverpool and a Yachtmaster Examiner. His own boat is a Squib, which he races with his family in North Wales. He also sails in larger yachts offshore, as a relief skipper with the Ocean Youth Club.

IAN McLAREN is also a professional seaman, a lecturer in navigation in London and a Yachtmaster Examiner. His own yacht is a Nicholson 26, in which he and his wife have made many long voyages, including passages to Spain and the Azores.

BILL ANDERSON, the RYA Cruising Secretary, is the member of staff responsible for the Yachtmaster training and examination schemes. He was trained as a navigator in the Royal Navy and sails with a young family from the Solent.

Grateful acknowledgement is made to the Controller, HM Stationery Office, and the Hydrographer of the Navy for permission to reproduce details of British Admiralty charts included in this book.